PAY DIRT

Divorces of the Rich and Famous

The unauthorized inside stories of the nation's
20 most sensational divorces

by

James A. Albert

Branden Publishing Company, Inc.
Boston

©Copyright 1989
by James A. Albert

Library of Congress Cataloging-in-Publication Data

Albert, James A.
    Pay dirt : divorces of the rich and famous / by James A.
      Albert. p. cm.
    ISBN 0-8283-1927-8 : $17.95
    1. Trails (Divorce)--United States.   I. Title
KF226.A42 1989
346.7301'66'0269--dc20
[347.3061660269]

BRANDEN PUBLISHING COMPANY
17 Station Street
Box 843,Brookline Village
Boston, MA 02147

Contents

PREFACE

I began researching this book four years ago in the Los Angeles County Courthouse. I'd been thinking about it for months and had decided that readers would be as fascinated as I was by the behind-the-scenes stories of some of the most sensational divorces ever fought out.

I was convinced that such a book would be entertaining to read and enjoyable for me to research. This was going to be fun, and I was excited to begin. So, at 9 a.m. on a sunny March day in 1985, I walked into the office of the L.A. Clerk of Court and requested the first volume of their computerized index of case files so I could begin my work.

It was not to be. I was brusquely told that the computer print-out was in use. I could have it in an hour or so. Then, I noticed a young file clerk seated at a desk behind the counter, obviously not quite ready to embrace the new day. He was bent over, napping, and his head was resting on that thick computer index! He was using it as a pillow.

At that moment, I realized this research was not going to be as quick and easy as I once thought. But within an hour, Sleeping Beauty was awake, I had my index, and the investigation was underway. At the time, I never dreamed it would take four years to complete. I could never have done it alone.

This book simply could not have been written without the enthusiastic and competent help of several key people.

Karla Westberg, faculty secretary at the Drake University Law School, meticulously typed all of the numerous drafts of these chapters and was an insightful source of advice and encouragement all along the way. She has been my most essential partner in this from the first day.

A group of brilliant young attorneys for whom I have enormous respect and affection dug through thousands of pages of research material for these chapters while they were still in law school working with me. These stalwarts are Timothy N. Carlucci of Washington, D.C., Deborah S. Chang of Connecticut, Edward A. Gilkerson of Missouri, Patrick A. Kirchner of Iowa, Susan Burden Leonard of Wisconsin, James R. Overdorf of New York, Sheryl A. Soich of Iowa, Gary R. Urquhart of New Jersey, Daniel C. Voogt of Iowa and Constance C. Welu of Iowa.

Additional Los Angeles Courthouse research was vigorously and astutely conducted by hardworking law students Lawrence Walker, Dawn Whitney and Kevin Greenwood.

Back in Des Moines, a team of bright and energetic law students continued the extensive search for facts about each celebrity and their trials. Those proficient researchers, each of whom has since graduated and excelled, were Megan M. Antenucci, Kristy G. Arzberger, Charles C. Brown, Jr., Martha A. Fagg, Shannon G. Holz, August B. Landis and Kendall R. Watkins.

Drake University Law Library Director John Edwards, the resourceful law librarians at Drake and the librarians at Drake's Cowles Library all contributed to this book's extensive research base.

Sharon Malheiro, a former newspaper journalist who as a third-year law student is my invaluable and outstanding research assistant, expertly proofread the finished chapters and has been responsible for all pre-publication legal research.

Of course, there would have been no book without the vision of the publisher, Adolpho Caso, the distinguished President of Branden Publishing Company, Inc., with whom it has been a pleasure to work. We share an unyielding commitment to accurate and honest reporting.

I wouldn't have known many of the celebrities in these pages if my teen-age sons, Brian and Brad Albert, hadn't had the television on as much as they could every single day. And my parents, Mr. and Mrs. Richard Albert, have been behind me all the way.

When I began this research four years ago, I was a fan of each of these celebrities. I still am. Even more so. And I genuinely hope these upbeat stories of their triumphs over divorce inspire every reader.

James A. Albert
Professor of Law

Robin Givens, star of ABC's "Head of the Class" and her husband, Mike Tyson (in an arm cast). (Steve Granitz, Celebrity Photo)

Chapter 1

Mike Tyson

Mike Tyson brawled his way to the top of professional boxing to become, at 21, the youngest man ever to be crowned Heavyweight Champion of the World. From steamy, dimly-lit small town gymnasiums with sweat-stained canvasses to the opulent Las Vegas resort arenas, Tyson brutalized all comers.

He's a doomsday machine, with massive fists who atomizes opponents and leaves them flat on their backs in the center of the ring, out cold. As of February of 1989, he has won 36 straight fights--32 of them by crushing knock outs. He works fast, too. For instance, it took him just 91 seconds to knock out Michael Spinks in 1988.

Ironically, Tyson's longest and most difficult fight wasn't on any canvas. It lasted eight tortured months in 1988 and his opponent was Robin Givens, a 105-pound bantamweight with steel willpower and grit. The sensational bout was their brief, stormy marriage where Iron Mike finally met his match.

Let's go down to ringside for the introduction of tonight's fighters.

In the near corner, wearing black trunks and black shoes without socks, weighing in at 220 pounds, from the streets of Brooklyn, New York, the Heavyweight Champion of the World, Mike Tyson.

As a kid, Mike was a street punk, from the roughest part of town. He mugged women and stole their jewelry, ripped purses from the hands of old ladies and held up shopowners with a .22 caliber pistol. His own sister, Denise, told Sports Illustrated reporters that "it became fun for him to beat up kids." While still a child, he was arrested 38 times and confined to a series of juvenile detention centers in Brooklyn. Incorrigible, he was finally sent away to a reform school in upstate New York when only 12 years old.

One of Mike's counselors was a former boxer and introduced him to an aging boxing manager, Cus D'Amato, who lived nearby. D'Amato, a grizzly Burgess Meredith-type trainer, was known for turning tough kids from prison and reform school into professional fighters. Floyd Patterson had been one of his proteges years before.

D'Amato took one look at the angry 200-pound manchild with steam spraying from his nostrils and took the boy in. The year was 1980. The old man's Catskill training camp was like a military barracks--the facilities were spartan and D'Amato demanded that the street toughs paroled to him obey his discipline.

But D'Amato opened his heart to young Mike and took him under his wing. He offered to become Mike's legal guardian. For the first time in his life, Mike had someone who believed in him and who knew how to transform him. While there, Mike actually attended eighth and ninth grades at the Catskill High School and slowly began to calm down. He spent hours every day in training, under D'Amato's watchful eye, and listened attentively as the old man lectured and taught him the complete science of boxing. He was learning the sport at the feet of a master and became, quite literally, a student of boxing.

Mike watched old newsreel footage of past prizefights and studied everything that had been written about the greatest fighters in history. In the gym, D'Amato developed and fine-tuned every facet of Mike's boxing--physical and mental. He taught him how to overpower opponents mentally and destroy them with his huge fists. Over the span of six years, concentrating on one part of his body at a time, the old man built Mike Tyson--almost bionically--into an unbeatable fighting machine. They would call him "Iron Mike." He calls himself "the baddest dude on the planet."

Not that D'Amato drained any of Mike's anger out of him--he channeled it into the ring and aimed it at the opponent. Mike admitted to Sports Illustrated eight years later that "I love to hit people. I want someone to attack me. Just me and him. I like to beat men and beat them bad."

Turning pro in 1985, Mike knocked out his first 19 opponents--13 of them in the first round. In 1986, he KO'd Marvis Frazier in 33 seconds and had everyone in boxing talking. He won the heavyweight championship later that same year by demolishing Trevor Berbink. He was the youngest champ in the history of the sport.

A Sherman tank in trunks, he threw blows with both hands and could lift a 200-pound man off the canvas with one of his powerhouse uppercuts. He took no survivors. The night he pulverized Jesse Ferguson and knocked him out cold in the sixth round of a major 1986 bout, he growled to reporters that "I wanted to drive his nose bone into his brain." He went on to knock out Tyrell Biggs in short order, former heavyweight champion Larry Holmes in four rounds and WBA champion Tony Tubbs in six minutes. And in June, 1988, he pummeled former champ Michael Spinks in a title bout and knocked him out in just 91 seconds.

Along the way, he became the richest athlete in history. His take from the Spinks fight alone was $21 million, HBO paid him $26 million to televise seven of his bouts and Pepsi Cola ponied up with $4 million for Mike to star in just one of its 1988 commercials. Some people say he's worth $50 million today.

In the far corner, wearing sleek designer dresses and pricey jewelry, weighing in at 105 pounds, from the most expensive private finishing schools and colleges in the East, the challenger--Robin Givens.

Robin is a brilliant, attractive overachiever who is a near perfect person. Just ask her. "I'm almost rational to a fault," she gloated to the New York Times. As a teen-ager, she was not only a beautiful model but an outstanding student as well. Quite refined and cultured, she studied music and dance. She entered the Ivy League's fashionable Sarah Lawrence College at age 15--when most of the rest of us were still trying to learn our locker combinations in tenth grade. When only 19, she entered the Harvard Medical School, but dropped out two semesters later when she was discovered by Hollywood and offered an acting career.

In a television role just meant for her, today she stars as Darlene Merriman, a snooty superbrain in a high school class for gifted students on ABC's *Head of the Class*. But not everyone gives Robin high grades.

The Harvard Medical School, for instance, says she was never a student there. Nor were her days at Sarah Lawrence well remembered--her classmates despised her. In fact, she was the only senior to be publicly booed at graduation. Delores Robinson, the mother of Holly Robinson, one of Robin's classmates at Sarah Lawrence who now stars in Fox TV's *21 Jump Street*, told Newsday reporters that "everybody hated Robin. She's a manipulative, scheming opportunist." Brian Robbins, one of her ABC costars, lamented to People magazine that she was "abrasive and vicious." That same magazine quoted an unnamed acquaintance of Robin's from college as revealing "she's really not a very nice girl. She goes after what she wants no matter what the price."

Robin didn't fight solo--she had a tag team partner in her attractive, middle-aged mother, Ruth Roper. They were inseparable, and Ruth's influence over her daughter was amazing.

Life magazine quoted Roper as saying she'd raised Robin to be "smart, beautiful and gutsy--everything that can be intimidating to a man." The unusual thing was that even after Robin left home, Ruth stuck like glue and acted as her constant companion, adviser, confidante and spokesperson.

ROUND ONE

Watching television one day, Iron Mike noticed pretty Robin and asked intermediaries to arrange a dinner date so he could meet her. In early 1987, a rendezvous was organized at a trendy Los Angeles restaurant and the champ flew to California. Robin was waiting at the restaurant, but she brought her mother along too, to be with them for the evening. It was all right with Mike, who was awed by Robin's beauty and flair, and who asked her out several times after. She seemed to turn her nose up at him at first.

They had some dates, but Mike confided to Life magazine that "I felt like a peasant trying to date the queen's daughter."

ROUND TWO
    Their relationship was "on again/off again" for months. After a spat with Robin in June, Mike was quoted by Los Angeles Times reporters as confiding that "I'm never going to get married. These women are all just after my money. If I wasn't rich and famous, they wouldn't want no part of me, and I know it."

ROUND THREE
    Eight months later, on February 7, 1988, Mike and Robin were married in a Catholic Church in Chicago. It was spur of the moment, without even a marriage license, so they had to make it legal two days later in New York City in a 90-second civil ceremony. The groom was 21 and the bride was 23. Robin made one thing very clear to Mike before the wedding--she and her mother came as a package. Where Robin went, Ruth went--even into a marriage. It was going to be Three's Company with Ruth right in the middle of it.
    In so many ways, though, Robin Givens and Mike Tyson are the 1980's Odd Couple. She graduated from a prestigious Ivy League college, he is a ninth-grade drop-out. She is a whiz kid and genius, he isn't overly book-bright. She is worldly and sophisticated, he is naive and crude. She is articulate and well-spoken, he murders the Queen's English. She is stunningly beautiful, he is rough looking with several teeth missing.
    Was it true love that forged this unlikely union, or was it more sinister? Eight months later, when the marriage folded, the National Enquirer reported that Robin's father believed she had married the champ to boost her acting career and get her hands on some of his $50 million so she'd be set for life. Reporters for that tabloid wrote that Reuben Givens felt his daughter was trying to wrap Mike around her finger, and that both Robin and her mother were

out to strip Mike of his manhood by ordering him around, telling him what to say, and even dictating what clothes he could wear. Sadly, as the marriage unfolded, many events seemed to bear dad out.

ROUND FOUR

In the spring of 1988, during the first few months of the marriage, Robin and her ever-present mother moved quickly to assert themselves and wrest control of Mike's career and money from his manager, Bill Cayton.

Cus D'Amato had died of pneumonia in late 1985 and Cayton had acquired Tyson's management contract. The reason Tyson fell to Cayton was that Cayton and his partner had bankrolled D'Amato to the tune of a quarter-million dollars which went to pay for Mike's room, board, clothing and training for all the years he lived with D'Amato. In return for Cayton having financially underwritten the young fighter, he held a contract giving him a one-third cut of everything Tyson might earn once he turned pro. It was nothing new--most boxers are obligated to pay their managers a percentage of their earnings.

Boxers' managers typically are responsible for keeping track of every cent their fighters earn and they handle all the personal banking. They speak for the boxer, enter into contracts on his behalf, negotiate for him and commit him to future fights. But Givens and Roper decided Cayton's cut was too big and they didn't want him calling the shots anymore. Newsday even reported that Mike was persuaded to sign over to Robin a full power of attorney over his fortune, which infuriated Cayton. At the same time, Roper's lawyer, Michael Winston, sent Cayton a letter demanding that Roper be given a full accounting of Tyson's fortune.

Even millionaire real estate tycoon Donald Trump, an enthusiastic boxing fan, joined in as Mike's personal adviser to help him break loose from Cayton's rich contract.

In the summer, Roper, Givens and attorney Winston showed up at the filming of Mike's $4 million Pepsi commercial and halted shooting. They took Mike off the set and wouldn't let him return until Cayton reportedly agreed to a pay cut from one-third to one-quarter of the Pepsi deal he'd put together. The entire film crew and 200 extras waited for three hours until Cayton finally gave in. As Cayton and Tyson initialed the new contracts, Robin gave a thumbs up sign to her mother. Tyson was brought back and the filming continued.

In all fairness to the active duo, Givens and Roper maintained all along that they were only trying to protect Mike and make sure that he never relinquished control of his finances to an outsider. They denied they were making a power grab and insisted he was the one who was unhappy with Cayton.

But sometimes their words and deeds gave people a different impression. For instance, when this battle was raging, the New York Times quoted Roper as stating "if I'm not involved, Michael doesn't fight."

ROUND FIVE

The struggle for the control of Iron Mike escalated in the summer when ostentatious boxing promoter Don King reportedly tried to get to Mike through his wife and mother-in-law. King told people no one could love Mike the way he could and was quoted by New York Post reporters as hissing that Cayton was a "vicious, lying SOB."

Without warning an hour before the June 27 Spinks fight, Mike had a process server slap Cayton with a lawsuit for the rights to his contract. Reeling, Cayton exploded that Don King was the one who was trying to break the contracts with his fighter and gain power over the world's richest boxer.

The feuding between Givens and Cayton never really let up, but after several months Mike's attorneys admitted that Cayton's management contracts were ironclad through 1992. The lawsuit was settled out of court with Cayton offering to accept only a 20% cut of Tyson's boxing earnings, but he would remain his manager.

In terms of the public's perception of Robin and her mother, however, the dirty little lawsuit was one more example of them trying to alienate Mike from his old friends and take over themselves.

ROUND SIX

Time to spend some of Mike's millions. A place in the New York suburbs would be nice, but who's going to pick it out? Roper, of course. And after a month-long search, she found a 30-room castle on 15 wooded acres in Bernardsville, New Jersey. Robin had wanted an estate and this one had eleven marble fireplaces and seven bathrooms. The neighbors--Malcolm Forbes, Jacqueline Onassis and Whitney Houston--probably wouldn't be bothersome. Mike paid the $4.5 million tab and his little family moved right in.

Living in the country takes wheels and they next acquired a fleet of luxury automobiles, including a $180,000 Bentley, a Rolls-Royce, a Mercedes convertible, a BMW 318-i and a black Porsche 924. The Tysons were always on the go, too, with Robin commuting to her Hollywood Hills home for the taping of her weekly TV show, Mike still maintaining his Catskills training camp upstate and the three of them jet-setting wherever business or fun beckoned.

ROUND SEVEN

But as the new marriage hit summer, the wheels came off. Mike and Robin were quarreling and the weirdest things started happening. Was Mike out of control? Had Robin been so obnoxious and overbearing that she pushed him over the brink? Or was he just a mad dog who went wild when she tried to tame him?

On May 8, as Mike was driving his Bentley from New York to the New Jersey compound with Robin and her mother, he suddenly swerved and crashed into a parked car. Police officers called to the scene were flabbergasted when Tyson threw over the keys and told them to keep the car for themselves because he'd had so many accidents with it. There were two versions explaining what had happened. The official line was that Mike veered to avoid hitting a stray cat. New York Times reporters, on the other hand, had it that while riding along, Robin found condoms in the champ's jacket pocket and flew into a rage, slapping him while he was trying to drive.

Tennis pro Stephanie Givens, Robin's sister, scoffed at the notion her sister was bashing Mike. Instead, she insisted, it was just the other way around--in real life, Mike was a wife-beater.

Mike's fists were sure working the night in August when former opponent Mitch "Blood" Green confronted him on a Harlem street. Green, who had lost a brutal 10-rounder to the champ earlier, taunted him at 4:30 a.m. outside Dapper Dan's, an all-night men's clothing store. A street brawl flared and Tyson broke Green's face. In the process, however, he fractured his own hand and was sent to the emergency room for a cast.

Mike could still drive a car, though, and in September smashed his wife's silver BMW into a huge chestnut tree on the grounds of his Catskill training camp. He was knocked unconscious and spent several days in the hospital. Roper reportedly took charge and ordered that Mike's manager, trainer and friends not be allowed to visit his sick room. The story then broke that it had been a suicide attempt and that Givens and Roper had called for a psychiatrist.

Again, there were two versions of the bout with the chestnut tree. Many believed it was truly a suicide attempt, brought on after Mike and Robin had been arguing for weeks. They say Mike literally begged Robin to leave her fancy New York City friends for a few days and join him at his training camp, and that she flatly refused to do so. At that latest rejection from his own wife, he bolted out the door for the BMW parked in the drive.

Mike himself offered the second version, denying there had been a suicide attempt. He told Reuters, the British News Service, "I have too much butt to kick in the ring to try and kill myself."

Whatever really happened, Iron Mike was uncharacteristically horizontal in the hospital and itching to get out. After four days and against doctors' orders, he jetted to Moscow to join Robin and Roper for the taping of the new season's premier episode of *Head of the Class*. While in the Soviet Union, Mike allegedly went berserk and chased Robin and her mother all over the hotel for four hours one bizarre night, threatening to kill them if he caught them.

For those who are concerned about the future of Glasnost and who think the U.S. is being too tough on the Soviets by sending them Givens, Roper and Tyson, rest easy that Mike returned in one piece after a week. But he quickly set his sights on . . . NBC. The day after landing back in America, an NBC News crew was attacked by the champ outside his New Jersey home. He threw his Walkman at them, tossed their camera to the ground and barked at them to leave him alone.

Right in the middle of all these strange happenings, promoter Don King, who never misses an opportunity to fawn over Tyson, mailed a two-page news release defending the champ to every boxing writer in America. Said the king:

> "(Mike Tyson) is a role model for our youth, an American hero for us all . . . . He represents America . . . . He is our ambassador of good will to all peoples of the world. Indeed, he is one of our national treasures . . . . Boxing needed a hero . . . and God sent Mike Tyson."

Thanks, Don, for putting things in perspective for the rest of us. But, does Iron Mike really have two personalities? Is he normal one minute and uncontrollably violent the next?

The side of him the public sees is warm and child-like. He's humble, simple and innocent. He's a softie--he gives beggars on the street $100 bills to buy food and he tenderly cares for 135 pigeons he keeps on the roof. The guy's a big teddy bear, warm and lovable.

But, is there any truth to the allegation that he's a Dr. Jeckyl and Mr. Hyde? Behind closed doors, is he a classic manic depressive with wild mood swings and deep depression? Was he frantically jealous when Robin was away? Is he so violent at home that he needs lithium to calm him? In total, is there a dark and ugly side to Mike Tyson that was unleashed on his young bride which made her life with him a horrible nightmare?

ROUND EIGHT

By September, psychological help was definitely indicated to save the seven-month marriage. Who to turn to? A marriage counselor? A psychologist? A clergyman? Not for these two. They'd go on ABC's *20/20* Friday, September 30, 1988 and be interviewed by Barbara Walters about their marriage and all the vicious rumors that were swirling. That's the ticket--a Barbara Walters encounter group where you bare your soul for millions of TV viewers sitting in their living rooms watching.

It was unbelievable. Iron Mike, the Heavyweight Boxing Champion of the World, sat on a sofa in a trance next to his bride and gently caressed her neck ... as she bad-mouthed and belittled him. When asked how their relationship was going, Robin snorted that "it's been torture. It's been pure hell. It's been worse than anything I could possibly imagine. I'm talking about every day it's been some kind of battle, some kind of fight."

She disclosed that Mike had an "extremely volatile temper" and a "side to him that's scary." Around the house, "he gets out of control, throwing, screaming." Then, she blurted out that Mike is a manic-depressive who transforms himself into an abusive zombie. When he acts strange like that, she said, he refuses to sleep and instead wakes her up in the middle of the night and chases and terrorizes her.

Mike's response? "This is a situation in which I'm dealing with my illness." He admitted that "she tolerates my shit and I love my wife," and assured her that if she ever did divorce him he'd give her every penny he had to his name.

ROUND NINE

The nationwide television audience was shocked that Tyson would sit so passively while Robin made a fool out of him. Later, though, the New York Post quoted Mike as saying that Robin and Ruth had made him take Thorazine and lithium to dope him before the TV program. Don King chimed in for the same newspaper, "that's how they emasculated Mike on that show--they did it through drugs."

If the champ had been drugged, they apparently wore off. Two days after the Walters interview aired, New Jersey police were called to Tyson's mansion when Mike started throwing chairs and an iron fireplace grate through the windows. Robin and Ruth had summoned the law to calm Mike down because he was destroying the place. Bernardsville Police Chief Thomas Sciaretta, on the scene, admitted he was prepared to arrest Mike if Robin signed a domestic violence complaint against him. She declined to and instead fled to her home in Los Angeles.

Two days later, Mike drove in to New York City and caused a major traffic jam when hundreds of fans mobbed him to show their support. Many chanted "get rid of her," referring to Robin, and "I'm manic, too." Cries of "come back to us" could also be heard.

In New York that day, Mike started fighting back. He admitted to reporters that he'd been angry on Sunday: "I took it [the iron grate] from the fireplace and threw it through the window. So what? I paid for it. It's my house."

Then, he made an appointment to be evaluated by one of the world's best known psychiatrists to get a second opinion on whether he was really manic-depressive. Up to that time, his wife and mother-in-law had sent him to Dr. Henry McCurtis of Harlem Hospital to be treated, as Robin said on TV, for manic-depression.

The new doctor, Abraham L. Halpern, a clinical professor of psychiatry at New York Medical College, examined the fighter and announced to the New York Times that he was definitely not manic-depressive and "showed no signs of a major mental disorder." In fact, Dr. Halpern conferred with Dr. McCurtis and told Times reporters that both were in agreement that Mike was not manic-depressive. Halpern explained that McCurtis had prescribed lithium on a trial basis to control Mike's moodiness but that he had never felt

Mike suffered from any psychosis or major mental condition, such as manic-depression.

Mike's side of the story slowly began to emerge. They apparently did fight a lot of the time, and Mike knew why. He was quoted by the <u>Amsterdam News</u> saying "she treats me like she's so much better than me. At 21, I'm the heavyweight champion of the world, but she never lets me forget she was going to medical school and only dropped out to become a TV star and make lots of money." There were even reports that Robin had a temper of her own and would try to kick Mike in the groin when she got mad at him.

The champ's friends went to bat for him, too. Former light heavyweight champion and New York State Athletic Commission Chairman Jose Torres was quoted in the <u>New York Daily News</u> as flaring to reporters that "he's no manic-depressive, he's being manipulated." Torres continued, "I'm not accusing his wife, but Ruth Roper is a dangerous woman. She now has complete control over Tyson." As Torres saw it, Mike was an innocent victim of "a diabolical plot" by Ruth and Robin to control his fortune. Mike's been "absolutely brainwashed," lamented his friend.

Robin's enemies came forward, too, to stand up for Mike. <u>Sports Illustrated</u> quoted Delores Robinson, Holly's mother, as lambasting Givens for the way she mistreated Mike: "The whole thing was a setup. Robin married him for the money . . . [and then] she started to discredit him."

<u>ROUND TEN</u>

On October 6 in Los Angeles, Robin laced up her gloves for the main event. On that day, she and her mother met with heavyweight divorce bomber Marvin Mitchelson and told him that they wanted to terminate the marriage. Mitchelson, although a lawyer by training, has definite barracuda and pit bull tendencies--he has made a career of going for husbands' throats in ugly divorce cases.

The following day, Robin filed a formal petition at the Los Angeles County Courthouse demanding that she be granted a divorce from her husband of eight months. She also asked the judge to issue a temporary restraining order against Mike to keep him at least 1,000 yards away from her L.A. home, the ABC studios and from her mother. Further, she requested that the judge order Mike not to molest, attack, strike or telephone her or Roper. Her plan was for the judge to transmit these orders to the Los Angeles Police Department for enforcement, apparently confident that their SWAT teams could fend off an enraged Iron Mike.

To bolster her case, she swore out a blazing affidavit in which she said Mike "has, throughout our marriage, been violent and physically abusive and prone to unprovoked rages of violence and destruction." She explained that "the most recent incident in which I was physically terrorized by Michael occurred on October 2, 1988. [The Sunday just after the *20/20* interview.] I was awakened by Michael's hitting about my body and my head with his closed fist and open hand." During that same fit, she remembers, "he started throwing dishes and liquor bottles at me, and he hit me with one dish which shattered all over me."

Robin stated that the incident on October 2 "was the latest in a continuous horror story for me. Michael has repeatedly hit me, threw things at me, threatened to kill me, and kill my mother...."

And, she contended that "Michael has been in treatment by several psychiatrists for manic-depression and other disorders."

Ruth Roper also wanted to be heard and she, too, filed a sworn statement with the court. In it, she recounted that, on their recent trip to Moscow, "Michael started going berserk." She reported that on their last night in the USSR, fueled by lithium and vodka, Mike "spent approximately four to five hours chasing me and Robin and Phyllis, a former employee of Robin's, around the hotel and throughout the lobby. When a Russian police officer attempted to intervene, Michael threatened to kill him, as well as the rest of us."

Even worse, Ruth claimed she had "on several occasions, personally witnessed Michael hitting and beating Robin." And, she added, "Michael has threatened me personally and threatened to kill me and have me killed."

Olga Rosario, one of the Tyson's house servants back in New Jersey, also supported Robin's claim that Mike was a violent beast. Ms. Rosario declared in an accompanying court document that "I have witnessed on numerous occasions, Michael's unprovoked violent outbursts." Particularly, she recalled his October 2 tantrum which began when he barked, "f--k you, you whore, you bitch" to her in response to her "Good Morning, Mr. Tyson" greeting to him. He then ran up onto the roof to brood and when Olga offered him his breakfast, "he just sat there and yelled at the top of his lungs, 'f--k you, f--k you.'"

After that, Olga reported, Michael indeed did hit Robin with a glass and destroyed all the glasses and dishes he could find. At that point, as Olga tells it, Robin had enough and said somberly, "Michael, I can't take this." The Bernardsville police were called, Robin, Ruth and Olga fled to California and the divorce papers were filed.

Attorney Mitchelson had the last word, in one of his trademark courthouse press conferences where he flashed some of his braggadocio for the TV news crews. "Tyson is emotionally disturbed--there's no question about it," he stormed, while threatening to take 50% of everything Tyson had, under California's community property law.

ROUND ELEVEN

Iron Mike wasn't about to let Robin and Mitchelson land all the blows, and he came out swinging. On October 14, he filed his own petition for divorce in Superior Court in Trenton, New Jersey. Then he asked the judge to annul his marriage to boot because Robin had tricked him into it by claiming she was pregnant. An annulment would cut Robin out of all of Mike's money because the judge would proclaim that the marriage never legally occurred.

Mike claimed that Robin hadn't ever really committed herself to the marriage for the long-term, but had been out to get his money quickly and then run. He said he "was the hapless victim of [Robin's] intentional fraud" and that she had maliciously tried to cut him off from his loyal friends and advisers during the marriage.

Citing the mean things she'd said about his mental health on national television, his suit charged she'd been extremely cruel to him and had attempted "to publicly humiliate . . . [him], strip him of his manhood and dignity, and destroy his credibility as a public figure."

Faulting both Robin and her mother for manipulating him all those months, the champ felt the marriage had actually hurt his career and subjected him to ridicule as some kind of Iron Wimp.

The filing in New Jersey was strategic, as Tyson's lawyer, Howard Weitzman, attempted to steer clear of California's potent community property laws.

Mike didn't confine his counterpunching to his lawsuit, however, and granted an interview with the Chicago Sun-Times in which he savagely took it to Robin. Robin and her mother "thought they were royalty," he scoffed, and claimed they wanted to be white and that "the way they talked about black people you'd think you were living with the Ku Klux Klan. . . ." Further, that "they didn't believe in people that broke their ass."

He said both women were after his money, but that he didn't blame them for trying. What angered him was "just the idea that they played the scheme on me. It was like a sting game. They worked on my emotions because I was in love. . . ."

What really hurt, Mike said, was that Robin didn't just stop at making a grab for his fortune, that she stuck the knife in and tried to ruin and embarrass him. And, he figured, "that was evil."

In other interviews, Mike denied beating his wife. "She'd disintegrate," he told several British reporters.

Several of Tyson's friends came forward to fill in other parts of the story of the eight month marriage. Sports Illustrated quoted Bill Cayton as remembering that it was Ruth Roper who was brandishing the shotgun and had telephoned Mike's managers with the news that Robin was 3 1/2 months pregnant.

ROUND TWELVE

The fans were quickly making up their minds about who should win this fight and it was a nearly unanimous decision. The *20/20* interview had left an indelible impression with millions of viewers of a hateful, mean-spirited Robin hitting her simple but nice husband below the belt while he sat calmly by. She was bombarded with threats, hate mail and widespread ridicule. The National Enquirer hurriedly conducted a nationwide survey and blared across its November 15th front cover that she was indeed "America's Most Hated Woman." Even Barbara Walters later acknowledged all the reports of intense adverse public reaction that showed Robin as "one of the most disliked" people in the country. Robin herself was pictured on the December 19th cover of People magazine next to the giant headline, "Why Does Everyone Hate Me?"

Some insiders are claiming it was in response to the wall of public contempt building against her and threatening her acting career, but Robin suddenly fired Marvin Mitchelson and announced she didn't want a dime of Mike's wealth. She retained New York attorney Raoul Felder, who told reporters that "Robin is waiving all claims. She will not be asking for nor will she take any money." Felder read a prepared statement from Givens giving up any claims to Mike's millions:

> "Michael can have his divorce. I never married Michael for his money. Therefore this represents no loss for me. At the cost of protecting him, I believe I sacrificed my marriage. I never wanted anything for myself."

At Felder's promise to drop Robin's California divorce within a day so Mike's New Jersey suit could sail smoothly through the courts, Mike's attorney proclaimed "complete victory." Said Howard Weitzman excitedly, "I consider this a Tyson knock-out."

Some observers didn't see it that way, pointing out that even if she did decline to take any of Mike's money, she never said she didn't expect a fair share of the marital prop- erty. At the top of that list of assets, of course, was the $4.5 million Bernardsville compound and the $2 million in jew- elry Tyson reportedly gave her during the marriage. She'll still walk away with a fortune.

Skeptics also questioned her true motivation and con- cluded she did it to avoid any more damaging adverse publicity. Her chances of landing future movie and TV roles might well have been jeopardized if she continued to squeeze Mike, and the public blamed her for it. Once the public pegged her a dislikable, selfish golddigger, no pro- ducer or director would ever touch her. So, she might have called off the dogs just to save her career.

Michael Elias, the co-executive producer of *Head of the Class*, immediately applauded Robin's move to renounce any claim to Tyson's wealth, telling the Los Angeles Times: "I really think that will help her image."

As the days and weeks wore on, though, it was clear Robin did want some money. In secret negotiations with Tyson's lawyers, her attorneys reportedly were demanding cash from the champ that they claimed was Robin's to begin with--$600,000 which she says she provided Tyson and $300,000 in fees from the Pepsi and Toyota commercials Mike did. From Mike's side of the bargaining table, his at- torneys were insisting on access to Robin's financial records and an accounting of nearly $2 million she had on hand which they claimed was mostly Mike's.

By the time in early November that Mike consented to an exclusive New York Post interview about his divorce, he had plenty to get off his chest. On November 7, the Post quoted him as saying that she "is continuing to manipulate the public. She manipulated me . . . Now it turns out she was lying when she said she didn't want anything from me."

Then, Mike was quoted as adding that "I gave her love-- and then she stabbed me in the back . . . and she stole money from me when we were together."

And the champ reportedly lashed out at the mother-daughter duo, calling them "the slime of the slime . . . mean and vindictive . . . . They tried to turn me into an imbecile. They got enough already from me."

ROUND THIRTEEN

Robin was outraged by what Mike told the Post and on November 16, slapped him with a whopping $125 million libel suit in federal court in New York. Arguing that Mike's statements were "false, defamatory, malicious and libelous," she contended going public against her in that way had been "heinous and inhuman treatment" on his part.

Her lawsuit claimed that because of Mike's harsh comments, she'd been "held up to public contempt, ridicule . . . [and] disgrace . . .; has suffered great mental pain and anguish; has been irreparably injured in her good name [and] . . . reputation . . .; and has lost the esteem and respect of her friends . . . and of the public generally."

Explaining her decision to strike back, attorney Felder intoned that it was a matter of personal dignity and that she'd turned her cheek too many times in their relationship already. Felder went on to tell the Washington Post, "All he had to do is shut up and he would have gotten everything he wanted." Squaring her latest big-bucks lawsuit with her public disavowal of any interest in Mike's fortune, Robin's attorneys pledged that she would donate all defamation proceeds to charity. As Felder emphasized in a Cable News Network interview, "we don't want his money. This [divorce] should be the simplest case that ever existed. And yet he throws one obstacle after another in front of finishing this thing off."

Tyson's attorney, Howard Weitzman, dismissed Givens' suit as a "laughable and ludicrous" publicity gimmick. He figured she deserved Mike's biting attack for secretly trying to soak him for money while telling the public she didn't want a dime. And, he told the Washington Post, Mike hadn't really tried to defame her. Rather, insisted the lawyer, "saying she's a slime is an opinion [and] he's entitled to his opinion."

ROUND FOURTEEN

Divorce makes strange bedfellows . . . and often shifts them around. For instance, after Robin left him, Mike Tyson fled to Don King's Cleveland training camp and remained sheltered there. King, who once so openly attempted to cozy up to Robin and Ruth, now blasts away at the women through press interviews, accusing them of hurting and betraying Mike.

After Mike moved in with him, King announced he and the champ had signed a four-year exclusive promotional contract. To that news, Bill Cayton swiftly replied that King's document was illegal because Cayton was still the fighter's only manager. Cayton vowed to sue King's pants off.

Donald Trump, of all people, took a slap at Tyson by firing of a sharp letter demanding $2 million for services rendered. In the letter, Trump reminded Mike that he'd agreed to pay that amount when Trump unleashed his killer lawyers on Bill Cayton to beat him into taking less of Mike's earnings. Trump calculated his intervention, which had been in concert with Robin and Roper, would save Tyson $50 million over his career. Trump vowed to donate the $2 million to charity. (Charities could come out very well in this divorce.)

The New York Times quoted Kevin Rooney, Tyson's long-time trainer, as shrugging at the latest developments: "Don King is worse than Robin Givens and Ruth Roper. They're bad. He's worse."

Some of Mike's friends say that with Robin and her mother out of his life, he can return to boxing--a gentler pastime. The Los Angeles Times quoted former heavyweight champion George Foreman as saying, "You can be dethroned in your own home. A woman can bring you to your knees." He spoke from experience--he's been married five times.

By the winter of 1988, though, it was time for Mike to turn his attention back to boxing. He signed a deal to defend his championship against huge 6'3" English heavyweight Frank Bruno on February 25, 1989 in Las Vegas, and got busy trying to get his life in order.

In November, Tyson turned to Christ and had Jesse Jackson baptize him, with Don King at his side. In December, Mike fired old friend and trainer Kevin Rooney and started amassing a new Team Tyson to prepare for the Bruno fight. And on Valentine's Day, he and Robin finally flew to the Dominican Republic and got a divorce, officially ending their marriage circus. As he and Mike walked away from Givens, King gloated "Free at last, free at last." Still to come, however, was the battle over money between Robin and Mike, and their lawyers agreed an audit should be done before going any further.

The big question in Las Vegas as the Bruno fight approached was whether his turbulent marriage to Givens had weakened the Champ. Everybody was buzzing about it; Bruno supporters were banking on it. But Tyson himself dismissed the fear, telling CNN just before the match that "It's behind me" and "I'll always be all right."

More than Bruno could say a few minutes later as Iron Mike loosened his head with a flurry of uppercuts and haymakers. As blood gushed from the challenger's mouth and nose, the referee ended the fight three minutes into the fifth round and awarded Tyson a stunning TKO.

After being bashed by his spunky wife for several months, Mike walked out of that Las Vegas ring a winner again. He and Robin will square off once more, of course, and the final round between them is bound to be a potboiler.

When the decision is in, hopefully each can go their separate ways and find peace and happiness in their lives.

But under the scorching ringside lights of the Las Vegas Hilton in February, one thing was clear. After his explosive and devastating marriage to Robin Givens, defending the World Heavyweight Championship against the second toughest and meanest boxer in the world was a piece of cake for Iron Mike.

ROUND FIFTEEN

Joan Collins, star of "Dynasty" at the Breeder's Cup Ball at the Beverly Hilton Hotel. (John Paschal, Celebrity Photo)

Chapter 2

Joan Collins

Joan Collins, the British seductress whose torrid and highly publicized affairs, marriages and divorces scandalized that nation for 25 years, steamed the windows of the Los Angeles County Courthouse in 1987 when she divorced her fourth husband, Peter Holm, who she considered an unfaithful goldbricking Swedish gigolo. After only 13 months of marriage, Joan wanted out; and her reasons became shockingly clear during the trial. As the Judge heard allegations of spectacular sexual escapades, wags gasped that the whole sordid affair couldn't have been more outrageous if *Dynasty* scriptwriters had concocted it as a series plot.

Her many fans should not have been surprised, however, that Joan's latest divorce devolved into more of a sex scandal than a quiet nipping of tender matrimonial bonds.

The lady is, after all, a flamboyant international sex symbol. As *Dynasty's* Alexis Carrington Colby Dexter, she portrays with flourish one of TV's most lustful, glamorous and sultry characters. Alexis is admittedly conniving, bitchy and evil, but her sex drive never falters as she swaggers from one sizzling bedroom scene to another.

In 1983, she posed nude for a salacious <u>Playboy</u> photospread and proved that a 50-year-old could indeed betoken sexual eroticism as she flashed her wares. In fact, one of the <u>Playboy</u> photographers observed: "There's a little bit of animal in her that she lets sneak out. You feel as if you're with a panther."

She was never well caged. At 19, Joan married famous British actor Maxwell Reed, a notorious cad who ravished his young flower. She walked out on him five years later after he reportedly made a deal with a wealthy Arab sheik who asked to rent Joan for one night in bed for 10,000 pounds. Then, she had a passionate affair with baby-faced 22-year-old Warren Beatty, whose own adolescent sex drive was so intense they made love up to five times a day. She was married to actor and songwriter Anthony Newley for seven years and to Beatles record producer Ron Kass for eleven, until Joan's spokesman claims she found out he was showing nude photos of her to his buddies and bragging about their sex life. Every marriage was stormy, each divorce scandalous. In between were randy trysts with some of the world's most eligible young bachelors, including Ryan O'Neal, Nicky Hilton and Sydney Chaplin.

Her own hot tell-all autobiography, *Past Imperfect*, sent such shock waves throughout England in its first release that its behind-the-covers bedroom scenes had to be toned down before publication and distribution in the United States. In it, she succinctly describes what it was like for a young movie actress living and working in Hollywood: "Sex was the best indoor sport going." Phyllis Diller once even quipped at a Dean Martin roast that "Joan Collins has whitecaps in her waterbed." Indeed, her whole adult private life has been a paradigm of prurience, and she has openly flaunted it.

On screen, her life has been equally notorious. She starred in several British soft-core porn flicks, including *The Bitch*, *Nutcracker*, and *Homework*. In *The Stud*, she played a nymphomaniac in the film adaptation of younger sister Jackie's fiery novel about seduction.

Voluptuous and sensual, Joan appears a spicy tart; and through more than 50 films earned the nickname "The British Bombshell" in the overseas press.

In 1981, at the end of its first season on television, *Dynasty* stumbled in near the bottom of the national Nielsen ratings. Its producers decided that the cure for the night time soap's anemia was to quickly infuse sex and wickedness into the show in the form of a new character who would portray Blake Carrington's ex-wife. Of course, when it came to nasty girls, Joan Collins had spent a career redefining the term and she was the instant choice to play Alexis. Joan was certainly up to acting greedy and bitchy, admitting to the Los Angeles Times that "I like playing Bad Girls." She went one step further with Playboy interviewers, telling them "I like women with balls, with guts." Well, Alexis Carrington Colby Collins, come on down!

Since bursting onto the scene, Alexis has connived, manipulated and double-crossed her way through every plotline. Consumed with wealth and power, she's ruthless with everything she does and everyone she touches. Fueled by animal-like lust, she plays with and then conquers weaker males in bedrooms, bathrooms, boardrooms and the backseats of Bentleys.

It is a role made for Joan and which she plays exquisitely. The Alexis character jumpstarted *Dynasty* and within a few months transformed it into one of the most popular TV programs in America. And for the first time in her career, Joan became a real star. After all the tough years grinding out unappreciated B and C movies, she is on top. She commands $50,000 per *Dynasty* episode and also earns hundreds of thousands of dollars from her endorsements of such Alexis-related products as Revlon's Scoundrel perfume and her own lines of elegant jewelry and lingerie.

While *Dynasty* was propelling her professional life to dizzying heights, her eye for young, firm men forced her into a personal life misstep in July, 1983. At a London pool party, she spotted handsome Peter Holm and innocently began another scandalous descent down the slippery slope of love.

At the end of the slide three years later, Peter would vividly describe their first meeting in court documents. Joan was attracted to him and asked if he'd escort her to the premier of *Superman: The Movie* that night. He enthusiastically did and after the show they went to a disco "where we danced together all through the night. This was the evening in which I fell in love with Joan. We had both fallen in love," as he explains it. He remembers that she left the next morning for Los Angeles and that her last words were that he should come to America and visit her. Joan could pick them, all right. In the sixties he'd been a tight-pantsed teen rock star in his native Sweden and was now a 36-year-old stallion, measuring in at 6'2," with a trim and muscular body and a tousled mane of curly blonde hair. They missed each other so intensely during the next two days that he agreed to fly to her in Hollywood later that week.

Once in America, Joan insisted Peter stay with her in her Beverly Hills mansion and took the young wide-eyed Swede for glamorous and romantic nights on the town to the finest restaurants and even to a posh party at the Playboy mansion where they danced until morning. She gave him a private tour of the *Dynasty* set and for three weeks they were "together all of the time." Peter also stated that during those first lust-filled days of their new relationship "we made love for the first time and we got to know each other more and more."

When he finally had to return to London to tend to his business selling telephone answering machines, Joan couldn't stand being apart and jetted across the Atlantic within a week to be with him again. He recalls that it was then that they decided they never wanted to be separated again, and so he sold his business and moved to America with Joan.

They lived together first for two steamy years, finally married in November of 1985, survived 13 months of turbulent wedlock and then ran to the Los Angeles County Courthouse--she for a divorce and he for $960,000 in yearly alimony from her. The court file tells their amazing love story.

According to Peter's own revealing statements, they were right in the middle of the frenetic Hollywood social swirl. Home was a fashionable toft at 2220 Bowmont Drive in Beverly Hills where they'd host intimate get togethers with stars like George Hamilton and Elizabeth Taylor who would join them on the sofa in front of the television to watch Joan in her series. They'd throw a party at their place every ten days and a major bash monthly where Russian caviar and smoked salmon would be served and champagne hauled in by the crate. A full-time maid, cook, gardener and four other household employees busied themselves taking care of Joan and Peter.

Despite the luxury and pampering which they enjoyed at home, they preferred to be out on the town or, more accurately, out on the world partying. They dined out at elegant Los Angeles restaurants five or six nights a week, typically spending $200 for their meals each night. After dinner, they'd go dancing "in the most sophisticated night clubs and discos in the world," as Peter tells it.

They had six cars with which to get around town, including a Rolls Royce and two BMWs, and "were always part of the local Hollywood party scene and attended, for example, parties at the homes of, or with: Johnny Carson, Linda Evans, Sammy Davis, Jr., Kirk Douglas, Morgan Fairchild, John Forsyth, Zsa Zsa Gabor, Larry Hagman, Julio Iglesias, Don Johnson, Lisa Minelli, Farrah Fawcett and Ryan O'Neal," again quoting from Peter's court account.

But the Hollywood scene often bored them and staring at the same forty walls at home would get to be a drag. So, they went jetting all over the world searching for excitement and pleasure. During their marriage, they stayed at the world's most expensive hotel, the Ritz in Paris, for three months at a cost of $200,000. They vacationed in Hawaii, Acapulco, the Caribbean and throughout Europe, typically staying in the Presidential suites of the finest hotels. When on the road, they chose their company selectively. President Reagan and Queen Elizabeth II entertained them, they joined Roger Moore for a ski vacation in Switzerland and, for their honeymoon, flew to meet and dance with Prince Charles and Lady Di.

Joan and Peter especially enjoyed the Continent and purchased two vacation homes in Port Grimaud on the southern coast of France, flush on the Mediterranean, and equipped their hideaways with a thirty-eight-foot yacht for romantic nights at sea.

They always traveled in style to the exotic locales on their vacation itineraries, flying in private jets all over Europe, by helicopter to the more secluded destinations and creating quite a stir on international commercial flights by appearing at airports with 40 pieces of luggage and their own computers, VCRs, large screen TVs and personal gymnasium equipment.

Back in Los Angeles, they went through millions of dollars during their year-long marriage. In 1986, Joan decided to buy a second Beverly Hills home and plunked down $2 million in cold cash for it. Located at 1196 Cabrillo Drive, the mansion boasted a separate guest house on the grounds, swimming pool, fountains and terraced walkways. The estate provided an awesome panoramic view overlooking Los Angeles and on clear days, Joan and Peter could see the Pacific Ocean several miles away.

Peter remembered that "shopping was one of our favorite pastimes" and that they both enjoyed buying new clothes. In fact, he explained that it wasn't only that he liked shopping for clothes, but that his "public image" demanded that he dress "stylishly" at all times. Records show he spent $20,000 a month on new clothes and topped off his outfits with $400 alligator shoes.

Joan earned $5.2 million during the marriage to pay for their delirious pace, and it's not surprising they were featured several times on *The Lifestyles of the Rich and Famous*. She was truly a good provider and claimed she paid Peter a salary of $1.2 million for the first year, took care of $700,000 in expenses which he ran up and even gave him a $5,000 allowance each month in cash so he'd have pocket change.

Despite their wealth and the vast material possessions which surrounded them, it began to appear to some observers within six months of the wedding that Joan and Peter were not really happy together. Crew members caught glimpses of the two arguing heatedly on several occasions during the filming of the *Monte Carlo* miniseries including one time when Joan's temper exploded and she yelled at Peter to shut up because he didn't know anything about anything.

A major source of the trouble between them appeared to be Joan's slow burn over the fact that she had to get up at dawn every day to slave on *Dynasty* while Peter lounged at home with four servants.

As the months wore on, their bickering and fighting around the house intensified. Former servants were quoted telling horror stories of the two arguing from morning until night and then starting in on it all over again the next day. In the end, Joan tired of breaking her back to bring home the bacon and she invited Peter to the Warner Hollywood Studios one crisp December day to have an intimate lunch. He couldn't resist and as he drove his luxury sports car up to the studio, a stranger standing nearby walked up to the car and shoved a package in Peter's lap. "What's this?" asked the Swede. "Your divorce papers," snorted the process server.

On December 6, 1986, Joan filed for divorce, but the several pages of affidavit testimony which she attached to her petition read more like a lurid chapter from one of her sister's sizzling novels. She explained she wanted a divorce because "during the last several months, Respondent [Peter] has demonstrated a capacity for violence and irrational behavior." Describing him as 6'2" tall, weighing 185 pounds and having "imposing physical strength" she admitted being fearful for her safety and asked the Judge to issue a temporary restraining order against Peter so he couldn't harm her.

Joan proceeded to give the Judge specifics, claiming that Peter had literally thrown her 14-year-old daughter's nanny out of the house, shoving her to the ground and screaming profanities at her. The dazed matron promptly quit, of course. Another time, Peter became enraged when Joan's stepson parked in his space at the Bowmont house. As Joan tells it, Peter "screamed and shouted 'What the fuck do you think you are doing parking in my space?'" and kicked the lad out of the house and told him never to come back.

Joan asserted that Peter also came unglued when talking with a public relations agent, Justin Pierce, one day in Joan's dressing room at the studio. "He physically grabbed Mr. Pierce and said to him 'If you come around here again you're a dead man. I don't want to see your face. Get out. You're a dead man.'" And, Peter even turned on Joan, screaming at her in one rage and twisting her arm so forcefully that she was seriously hurt. She was so frightened that her heart began palpitating and her doctor rushed her in for an EKG. Reports Joan, "the doctor told me that I was suffering from extreme stress and anxiety."

She revealed that "these violent incidents upset me emotionally to the point where I cannot effectively concentrate on my work. I have been in a constant state of fear and depression." As an example, she recounted that she was a basket case on the *Dynasty* set December 5, 1986, making "frequent trips to my dressing room, where I cried. Several members of the crew expressed their concern." In demanding a restraining order from the Judge, Joan insisted that unless Peter was restricted she would be "unable to work, which will ... cause delay and great and irreparable harm to the Dynasty production."

Vehemently disputing Joan's allegations, Peter swore out his own testimonial affidavit in which he attempted to set the Judge straight. The Swede insisted that it was Joan who was violent and who frequently flew into rages around the house. Denying he'd ever twisted her arm, Peter maintained that what really happened was that Joan "struck me in the face with her open hand, screaming 'I hate you, get out of this house.'" As he explained it, it was only then that "in an effort to calm her down and prevent her from striking me again, I held her hands and calmly stated, 'Darling, please calm down.'"

The Judge believed Joan's version of the Saturday Night Fights and, on December 22, 1986, slapped an order on Peter formally restraining him from molesting or harassing Joan and her children. And, the Judge ordered Peter to stay away from the home on Cabrillo Drive where Joan was living and even from the Warner Hollywood Studios where *Dynasty* was filmed. Deathly fearful for her safety and not trusting Peter to comply with the order, Joan hired seven bodyguards. One armed guard stayed with her on the *Dynasty* set every day, two rode shotgun in cars preceding and following her Rolls whenever she'd drive to work or around L.A., and four guarded her home 24 hours a day.

Several of Joan's personal friends came forward to tell fan magazines and gossip tabloids that they were relieved

Joan had finally seen through Peter and pulled the plug on him. They described him as a phony and a fake who sponged off her and stayed with her only to set himself up financially.

Joan's 83-year-old father, Joe Collins, blurted out to People magazine that "I never liked him from the beginning." Pauline von Gaffke, a Swedish countess and former Holm paramour who claims to have spent $100,000 on him when they lived together, was quoted by Star magazine as saying "he's hardly done a proper day's work in his life. When he was with me, I paid for everything, right down to his socks and underpants."

Joan must've bought a few jockey shorts during her turn with him, too, because after she kicked Peter out, she stormed into Nieman-Marcus with a load of his clothes and demanded to return them because he'd bought them without her authorization. At first, the sales clerk refused to accept them because, after all, they had been worn for quite some time. But Joan was so emotional about it, the store caved in and gave her credit for the clothes.

She had servants box up the rest of Peter's clothes, including his 60 pairs of shoes, and move them back to the old house on Bowmont Drive. Then she changed the locks and stationed guards around the Cabrillo property to keep him out. Joan was the sole owner of both homes, and she agreed to let Peter stay in the Bowmont place until she sold it. He returned to Bowmont with his tail between his legs.

Within a few days, horror struck--Joan cut him off. She refused to pay him any more salary or allowance, told him he'd have to pay the maid and gardener himself or go without and notified the gas, electric and water utilities that she was not going to be responsible for any bills he ran up while staying in her home. With no job and no income of his own, Peter was desperate and he filed an application at the courthouse seeking $80,000 a month in temporary alimony from Joan to tide him over.

In a financial statement filed with the court, Peter itemized his monthly expenses as including $16,500 to rent another home, $1,900 for groceries, $7,000 to pay salaries to household servants, $1,300 for the monthly telephone bill, $200 for personal grooming, $12,000 for clothes, $6,000 for entertainment, $500 to pay limousine expenses, $4,000 for travel and $8,000 in cash for spending money.

He explained to the Court that he was requesting that much money so he could "maintain my standard of living which I have enjoyed ... during our marriage." After all, he figured, Joan was making enough to pay all his monthly expenses and still have money left over to continue her own elegant lifestyle.

A preliminary hearing was held on Peter's application on March 27, 1987, and again on April 8 with Judge Frances Rothschild presiding. Marvin Mitchelson, famed divorce lawyer to the wives of stars, represented Joan. Peter was represented by Frank Steinschriber, a pudgy scrapper who knew he had an uphill battle and a broke client on his hands.

Mitchelson opened the hearing by telling the Judge that Peter had been paid $1,200,000 during the brief marriage plus $900,000 for his expenses. And, he noted, Holm didn't have to pay a penny in taxes on all that money, either. Disputing Peter's need for $80,000 a month in temporary support, Mitchelson looked at the Judge and frowned, "it seems almost incomprehensible there would be no money left at all" from the more than $2 million he was paid.

But Steinschriber protested that Peter "literally is out of money at this point. He doesn't have money to go out and put gas in his car and buy food."

Mitchelson refused to believe it, belittling the Swede as a goldbricker. Moreover, he told the Judge that his own client was exhausted after filming her last *Dynasty* episode of the season and was leaving for Europe in two days to spend the next three months relaxing with her children on the Continent. Mitchelson announced boldly that his client wasn't with him in court that day and that she didn't want the Judge to decide anything for three months until she was ready to return to the States. He pleaded with the Judge that it would be cruel to spoil Joan's vacation by scheduling the final hearing on temporary alimony during her hiatus.

Peter's attorney protested that it would be wrong to make Peter starve another three months and deny him the chance to be heard in court on his emergency motion so that the regal Joan wouldn't be inconvenienced. And the worst part, revealed Steinschriber, was that he'd just been told by Mitchelson that Joan had sold the Bowmont house and that Peter would soon be evicted and out on the streets. He needed that temporary support now more than ever.

The Judge grew sick of the haggling and asked Mitchelson when exactly it was that Joan would return from Europe. "July 18, your Honor." Without even explaining the reasons for her ruling, Judge Rothschild continued the hearing over until July 20, letting Peter's application for emergency funds spin in the wind for three more months.

Peter and his attorney just couldn't believe it and within a month they were back in court in front of another Judge trying to squeeze some money out of Joan so Peter could buy groceries. In a statement filed with the Court, Peter groused "I have completely run out of funds" to support himself and pay his attorneys to continue representing him. He submitted a brief to Judge Kenneth Black reminding his Honor that judges grant wives temporary alimony as a matter of course while a divorce case is pending so the woman can continue living in the style she became accus-tomed to and so she can retain attorneys to adequately protect her rights. The reason temporary attorney fees are so routinely granted, he noted, was to assure that the woman whose husband files for divorce has competent le-gal counsel to fight for her share of the marital pie. If she wasn't advanced money for that purpose, the thinking goes, her husband's attorneys would walk all over her. And, the more complex the marital assets, the more important it is to pay temporary attorneys fees to the wife so her attorney can start working right away unraveling the financial cobwebs the husband has woven to cover up his true assets.

Peter put it to the Judge straight: don't treat me or my requests for temporary support and attorney fees any differ-ently than you do a woman who's been married to a pow-erful star.

Frank Steinschriber opined that Peter would never even be able to locate all the marital assets without the strong help of an attorney. He explained that Joan had earned in excess of $5 million in 1986 from 24 separate enterprises and companies; that she had created pension plans, trust funds and deferred compensation plans with the money; that she'd sunk $4 million in real estate; and that it was going to be a whale of a job to investigate, sort out and trace all the money earned during the marriage, which Peter had a right to do.

Steinschriber also complained to Judge Black that Peter was being forced to call on his attorneys more often because of Joan's meanness and refusal to cooperate. Just getting Joan to agree to a simple division of personal property had taken the lawyers days because of all the petty bickering and unreasonableness. Fighting over who should get such items as her daughter's wastebasket and Peter's chainsaw, the final division broke down this way: Joan got the wastebasket, kitchen stepstool, ladder and Christmas decorations. Peter got his hair dryer, the reclining massage chair, telephone answering machine, ironing board and steam iron, chainsaw, T-square and a sackful of assorted screws. She was obviously prepared to fight him tooth and screw; and Steinschriber begged the Judge for money so Peter could litigate the case on an equal footing with Joan.

On May 28, 1987, Judge Black dictated the following two sentence entry into the official case docket: "Matter is called for hearing with both counsel present. Motion is argued and denied." No explanation was given, but Peter was sent away from the courthouse empty-handed once more.

Peter knew he was living on borrowed time--his days in Joan's Bowmont home were numbered and he was out of money. Desperate after being turned away at the courthouse, he took matters into his own hands. If no judge was going to disturb Joan during her summer vacation in Europe, he decided he would himself. Purchasing a round-trip first-class airline ticket to London, where Joan was relaxing, he proclaimed for the gaggle of reporters who met him at the plane, "I'm here to haunt her. I'm here to haunt the Bitch." Those threats and accompanying photos of him stalking through the airport were carried on the front pages of the London newspapers, as was his vow to spend a whole week turning London upside down to find his BMW which he claimed Joan was hiding there. Offering a $1,000 reward to any Londoner who helped him locate his car, he stomped off in hot pursuit of his bride.

He didn't find her, but the British press was having a field day covering the spat and he surely got her attention. Later, while still in Europe, Peter leaked word that since Joan wasn't paying him any temporary support, he was going to raise money himself by opening up her Bowmont Drive home to L.A. tour buses and charge admission for visitors to walk through the bedroom where the two of them had consummated their love.

That threat got to her. Furious, she ordered Marvin Mitchelson to do something about it before Peter returned to the States. Mitchelson responded by staging a raid on his client's home. Backed up by two Beverly Hills Police squad cars, several of Joan's own bodyguards and a locksmith, Mitchelson burst into the home, kicked out a very stunned buddy of Peter's who was housesitting, moved out all of Peter's belongings except the bed and his dirty socks, and changed the locks so the Swede couldn't get back in.

The invasion was only a temporary victory because when Peter returned to L.A. on June 26 he obtained a court order forcing Joan to honor her agreement to let him stay in her home until the new owner took possession. The Judge ordered Joan to let Peter back in the home but he did permit her guards to remain on duty outside to prevent Peter from trashing the place or removing any of her valuables during his last few days there.

July 10 was the date the new owner was entitled to possession of the premises. Peter first threw some wild, noisy parties at the house and lived it up. But as the deadline drew nearer, he got his back up and threatened to shoot anyone who tried to evict him. Holed up inside the mansion Alamo-style, Peter yelled out to startled reporters that he was armed and ready to fight to stay there. Joan obtained two separate court orders requiring him to vacate, but he refused. Armed police were dispatched with orders to secure the home and bodily remove him. They rolled toward Bowmont Drive.

Just minutes before the police arrived for the confrontation, Holm gave up his siege and came out of the house voluntarily. He did have some words for Joan and the waiting press, though. The next day the London newspapers quoted him as saying: "I shall shoot that bitch Joan. I'll pull the trigger. There will be a bloodbath."

On July 16, Peter and two of his friends picketed outside Joan's Cabrillo Drive home, blocking the driveway. Peter carried two large placards--one in each hand--which read "Is There One Law for a Soap Opera Actress and Another for the Homeless?" and "Be Fair; Peter helped You Get Rich; Give Holm a Decent Home."

Joan was unnerved by the Swede's public threats to shoot her, the ugliness he showed in marching in front of her secluded home and his repeated warnings that there were explosives in a bag he always menacingly carried. On July 17, with the trial to start in just three days, she and her attorneys took their evidence of Holm's harassment and threats to Judge Robert Schnider. Joan was afraid Peter would try to hurt her or kill her at her deposition which was scheduled for July 19 or at the trial itself in the crowded Los Angeles County Courthouse. William Glucksman, one of Joan's attorneys, stated this about Peter: "His conduct is indicative of a crazed, irrational maniac. He is out of control."

Judge Schnider quickly agreed and took strong measures to deny Peter the opportunity to carry out any threats. His Honor figured the batallion of uniformed Sheriff's deputies and Bailiffs would secure the courtroom and prevent any violence there, but he was concerned for Joan's safety on Sunday night before the trial when she had to present herself at the offices of Peter's attorney to have her pre-trial deposition taken. The Judge ordered that Joan be

permitted to bring up to five bodyguards with her to the deposition and that they would "have the right to conduct
searches, including body searches of Respondent [Peter]
and [his] agents other than counsel."

So that Peter couldn't scream that the rules were one-
sided, Judge Schnider also allowed someone representing
Peter "to conduct a weapons search of Petitioner [Joan]" at
the deposition. It must be emphasized that it is absolutely
unheard of for a judge to order or allow a body search of a
party before a civil deposition. That such an intimate and
intrusive invasion of one's body is permitted to be conducted by the adverse party rather than some neutral judicial officer is even more shocking. But Joan had clout, her
attorneys knew what they were doing and Peter had given
them sufficient evidence through his macho mouthing off to
somewhat justify such an otherwise offensive order.

On top of that, Judge Schnider ordered Peter to keep
himself and his placards at least 750 yards away from
Joan's home and the *Dynasty* set.

Finally, the Judge enjoined Peter from annoying or harassing Joan in any manner, directly or indirectly.

To effectuate the firm action he took, Judge Schnider
dispatched copies of his order to the Los Angeles County
Sheriff and Los Angeles Chief of Police with directions that
they immediately take the steps necessary to enforce every
provision in it.

The bitterness of their pre-trial sparring set the stage for
the main event--a four round championship divorce fight
held in the Los Angeles courtroom of Judge Earl F. Riley.
Gaveled to order on Tuesday, July 21, 1987, the trial exploded with such scandalous allegations, case-busting surprise witnesses and below-the-belt rabbit punching that,
after four long days of slugging it out, it was heralded as the
divorce trial of the decade.

Peter's attorney, Frank Steinschriber, opened with guns
blazing when he demanded for his client 50% of all the income Joan had earned during the marriage and $80,000 a
month in temporary support. He argued that under California law Peter was entitled to exactly half of all the money

that was earned during the 13-month coverture. Peter himself explained that he wanted an equal cut of the $5 million Joan brought in because she couldn't have earned it without him serving as her business manager and creative consultant.

The Swede remembered how he came to take charge of her business affairs: "As the days went by I had to comfort Joan as she had so many financial and business problems that were making her unhappy. I couldn't stand to see my sweetheart being unhappy." He negotiated the *SINS* mini-series with CBS, claiming credit as the program's executive producer for its ratings success and the mint that it made for Joan.

As Peter told it, Joan couldn't do anything without him. He said they had been "[i]nseparable. When Joan was in Europe, I was with her. We were always together. Every social function, private function, business function, we were always together." That $5 million was earned through their joint efforts, he insisted, and he wanted his half now.

And, as for his demand for $80,000 a month in alimony, Peter recited the list of his monthly expenses he'd prepared for Judge Rothschild earlier and threw himself on the mercy of the court as a homeless, jobless and helpless victim of a multimillionairess Hollywood star who, when she was done with him, had thrown him out and cut him off.

Joan's attorneys, Marvin Mitchelson and William Glucksman, ripped into Peter's testimony like a pit bull shreds a chunk of raw meat. They termed the $80,000 a month levy "an affront to the intelligence of this Court" because no Judge should be fooled into believing Peter was really penniless now since Joan paid him more than a million dollars in salary during the marriage. What happened to all that money?

Even more blunt in their censure of Peter's listing of monthly expenses, they claimed: "Mr. Holm's so-called 'needs' are absolutely ridiculous." Sniped Joan's lawyers, "Who is this man kidding?"

They called him a deadbeat, too. "Mr. Holm can work; he has just voluntarily chosen not to seek employment," they argued. It was Joan's belief that if Peter wanted to, he could easily land a high-paying job and start earning some money of his own rather than trying to leech off her while napping in his hammock all day.

Joan's attorneys emotionally argued to the Judge that "this case is nothing more than a contemptuous con-artist seeking to perpetuate his con on the judicial system by making a mockery of the support statutes ... and by attempting one more time to take advantage of a successful and famous movie actress."

When it came to disputing Peter's demand for half of Joan's earnings, Mitchelson and Glucksman didn't expend much rhetoric. They nailed him with one piece of paper. Calling Joan Collins to the witness stand on the first day of the trial, Mitchelson asked her if she and Peter had entered into any understanding about community property rights before their wedding. You bet, she assured him, and she explained how they'd written and signed a formal prenuptial agreement. Mitchelson brandished a piece of paper from his files--is this it? Yes it was--signed by both of us there at the bottom. Mitchelson had the document marked "Petitioner's Exhibit #1" and it was received into evidence by Judge Riley. It was brief and to the point and contained three separate provisions:

> 1.   During the marriage, Peter would be paid 20% of all of Joan's earnings.
> 2.   If they ever divorced, Peter would not be entitled to any California community property interest in any of Joan's income earned during the marriage. From the time of the separation on, Joan would get 100% of her earnings and Peter would get 0%.
> 3.   In the event of a divorce, Peter would abide by this agreement and not hire a lawyer to try to get more money out of Joan.

Joan testified that the terms were discussed and understood before they signed off and that she had insisted on such a contract before she'd agree to marry for the fourth time. She also told the Judge that she had not only lived up to her end of the deal, paying over to Peter 20% of all her earnings ($1.2 million), but had also paid $700,000 worth of charges which he'd run up for himself during the marriage. This guy had definitely not been a cheap date.

Mitchelson asked Joan point blank why she'd married Peter in the first place rather than continue playing house with him. Because "it would give him more status as a real man in my life ... not as a dog."

On the second day of the trial, Wednesday, Mitchelson called Edna R. Ruby as a witness. Ms. Ruby identified herself as the notary public who had witnessed the signing of this premarital contract on October 23, 1985. And who were the two people who signed this document in your presence? Why, Joan Collins here and Peter Holm sitting over at the other table. They signed it, legal and proper.

Mitchelson then argued to the Court that there were compelling reasons in addition to the prenuptial agreement for denying Peter any more of Joan's earnings. For one, the guy had bungled things so badly in handling the financial affairs that Joan now owed over $1 million in back income taxes. And on top of that, Lawrence Jay Turner, Joan's accountant, testified that Peter had become a millionaire under the prenuptial contract's clause paying him 20% of Joan's earnings. Peter had already walked away with plenty, said the accountant, after all Joan "is not a bank."

On Thursday morning it was Peter's turn again and he took the witness stand to testify on his own behalf. He had his work cut out for him explaining away that damning prenuptial agreement and the Judge listened intently as the Swede spoke slowly.

Peter admitted he'd signed the document, but argued he did so without consulting an attorney. He also claimed he was ignorant at the time about community property laws which would entitle him to a 50% cut. He explained that Joan was able to take advantage of him in the deal because he was Swedish and didn't have a command of the English words used in the contract, and because he'd never been married and never lived in California. Joan, on the other hand, had been divorced three times before and knew exactly how property and income were divided 50-50 at the time of divorce in California.

And, he disclosed Joan had demanded that he sign the agreement before she'd consent to marry him. As his attorney argued to the Judge, Peter had thus signed it "under extreme pressure and influence."

In his cross-examination of Holm, Marvin Mitchelson asked an interesting and seemingly benign question about whether Peter had been faithful to Joan. What if someone were to say he'd had an extramarital affair and concocted a plot to drain Joan financially and then drop her for his secret paramour? Straightfaced, Peter replied indignantly that would be "absolute rubbish." Mitchelson left it lay and politely excused Peter from the witness chair.

Peter's attorney then rested his case and the Judge turned to Mitchelson expecting him to do the same. At that point, just as TV's Perry Mason had done in hundreds of cases before, Mitchelson shocked everyone in the courtroom by calling a surprise witness to the stand who had been hiding outside in an anteroom. "I call Romina Danielson," he intoned to a hushed gallery.

Toward the front of the courtroom wiggled a strikingly gorgeous 23-year-old dressed in a white hat and a white skintight dress with a zipper all the way down the front. She was so hugely endowed physically that the word "voluptuous" would never do her justice. This was a true stunner clicking toward the witness stand in loud leopard-skin spiked heels, and every eye was on her.

Under delicate and even fatherly questioning by Mitchelson, Romina told a story of sex and intrigue so shocking that it blew Peter's case right out of the courthouse. In a little squeaky voice, Romina dropped the bomb that she and Peter had been having a lurid and secret affair which began while he and Joan were living together and which continued throughout 1985, the year in which he and Joan married. Peter was erotic, she explained. "There was just something about him ... the way he called me his 'Passion Flower.' The way he'd bring me roses all the time. The way he flattered me with his mouth."

She continued, "Peter told me I'm sexy and fantastic--that I have a way of making a man feel good. He was romantic. He called me his passion flower, his princess. It was just love, a romantic relationship, but I never condoned his lifestyle, what he was doing to Joan Collins."

What he was doing to Joan apparently was waiting until she left for a hard days' work at the studio and then bolting out of the house to rendezvous with his young and willing sex kitten.

Passion Flower also testified that Peter had confided in her his plan to use Joan for everything he could get out of her, to stay with her for two years and then dump her, and to take all the money and joint property he could from her. Admitted Romina: "He said he would get 50% of everything Joan had. He always talked about money."

She revealed that Peter told her he wanted her to bear his child "in a couple of years" right after he left Joan. Her voice getting weaker, she told Mitchelson: "We continued our ... sexual liaison through 1985. Then came a time when I thought I was pregnant ...." As she uttered the word "pregnant" her eyes spun around like windmills, her head bobbled and she fainted dead away.

Judge Riley immediately ordered a recess as the paramedics were summoned. Joan jumped up from her seat and strode triumphantly out the door as the whole courtroom exploded in hysterics.

The *Dynasty* scriptwriters couldn't have written a more spectacular ending to the trial.

As the hearing concluded the following morning, Judge Riley ordered Romina's testimony stricken from the record since she'd self-destructed before Peter's attorney had an opportunity to cross-examine her and challenge her allegations. The Judge then asked for closing arguments.

Frank Steinschriber, whose client was reeling after four days of revelations and repeated accusations that he was a cold, calculating con man, made one last attempt to persuade the Judge that it was Peter who had in fact been conned. He hammered away on the facts that Joan forced Peter into signing the prenuptial agreement against his will and that he really didn't understand what the document meant. Because of that, Steinschriber implored the Judge, the contract should be invalidated and Peter given his 50% community property share of Joan's income.

Marvin Mitchelson, in his argument, shifted the focus back to the Swede. Referring to him as the "con man," he reminded the Judge that Joan had already paid Peter nearly $2 million--"a lot for a 13-month marriage!" He continued degrading Peter with such remarks as "[h]e's a big, strapping fellow. If he wants more money, he can go out and earn it."

Mitchelson closed dramatically with these words which reiterated the gigolo theme of his case: "In their life together, he's gotten the maximum anybody could get. All he had to do was keep the books, drive nice cars, wear $1,300 suits and $500 silk shirts. Pardon my pun (looking directly at Judge Earl Riley)--that's the life of Riley."

After a four day trial and final arguments, the Judge had heard enough. He ruled from the bench that the prenuptial agreement was valid and that Peter was entitled to no more of Joan's earnings during the marriage. The Judge specifically found that "the agreement was understood by both parties; the agreement was executed without undue pressure or undue influence; [and] the lack of independent legal counsel was a deliberate choice of Mr. Holm."

When the Judge announced his decision, Joan began to cry and threw her arms around her attorney. Then, she waved triumphantly to the press outside and proclaimed "freedom from all entanglements forever."

Peter blamed the outcome on the devastating testimony of Passion Flower. Even though the Judge correctly ordered it stricken from the record, Peter grumbled "it still leaves a stigma."

Judge Riley refused to decide the questions of whether Peter should be granted any monthly alimony or attorney fees and set October 7, 1987 as the date for a final one-day trial devoted solely to those issues.

On August 25, 1987, Joan returned to the courthouse to routinely prove up her dissolution of marriage. Briefly taking the stand in Judge Kenneth Black's courtroom, she testified that irreconcilable differences had indeed developed between she and her husband to the point that they could no longer maintain their marriage. Peter was a no-show for the event, reportedly encamped in Europe; but Judge Black quickly granted Joan the formal dissolution which she sought, anyway.

Peter failed to appear at the October 7 hearing on his demand for alimony, too, and the Judge responded by denying his request and throwing his case out of court. A week later, Holm's attorney was back again, arguing that the Judge should reconsider his decision because Peter had a good excuse for missing the hearing--he was ill in France and unable to fly to Los Angeles. Holm then filed a request which reopened the case.

Joan, emotionally drained by Peter's relentlessness in seeking alimony, couldn't believe he was still harassing her. In February, 1988, the Judge finally put an end to it by awarding Peter a financial lump sum settlement of $180,000.

Joan went on to author *Prime Time*, a steamy novel about the behind-the-scenes rivalry between five actresses on a nighttime TV soap opera. Her book, an instant best seller, features characters with striking resemblances to Joan, her co-stars and her ex-husbands. While it sizzles with explicit heterosexual and homosexual bedroom scenes, it's still at least veiled fiction. And, if her marriage to Peter proved anything, it is that reality is stranger than fiction.

If Emmys were awarded for the most sensational divorce trial, Joan should win one for this. And a statue to Passion Flower as best supporting actress; with honors to Peter as best actor in a comedy role. They were a great cast. After all, their barbarous divorce lasted longer than the marriage itself.

AGREEMENT (IN ENGLISH) BETWEEN Joan Collins and Peter Holm
10/23/1985

PRE-MARITAL-AGREEMENT

1   This Agreement is made by reason of the Marriage that will
be entered between Joan Collins and Peter Holm.

2   All Gross income/earnings made by Joan Collins or any
Corporation(s) owned by Joan Collins shall be divided 80% to Joan
Collins and 20% to Peter Holm during the Marriage.

3   In case of a divorce: All Gross income/earnings made by Joan
Collins or any Corporation(s) owned by Joan Collins shall be
divided 100% to Joan Collins and 0% to
Peter Holm after the Marriage.

4   In case one party dies then this agreement shall be
considered null and void, and normal California Marriage Laws
shall apply as if this agreement had not been entered at all,
except that the surviving Spouse shall be the Executor of the
Estate.

5   Both Parties agree irrevocably to abide by this agreement
and to not become involved with Lawyers in case of divorce.

This Agreement entered 10/23/1985 at ~~2220 Bowment Drive B.H. CA~~
BEVERLY HILLS CA

-----------------------------   -----------------------------
        Peter Holm   Joan Collins

🄯 **SAFECO**
TITLE INSURANCE

STATE OF CALIFORNIA
COUNTY OF *Los Angeles* | SS
On this the   23 rd   day of *October*   1985, before me the undersigned, a
Notary Public in and for said County and State, personally appeared *Joan Collins and
Peter Holm*

                              personally known

———— proved to me on the basis of satisfactory evidence to be the
person ⌐ whose name ∂ are subscribed to the within instrument
and acknowledged that *they* executed the same.

FOR NOTARY SEAL OR STAMP

OFFICIAL SEAL
EDNA R. BUSY
NOTARY ...

Cher at the premier of "Torch Song Trilogy" in Century City
to benefit AIDS victims. (Scott Downie, Celebrity Photo)

Chapter 3

Cher

One of the funniest and most popular television programs of the early 1970s was *The Sonny and Cher Comedy Hour.* A special chemistry between the two stars made the show irresistible, especially Sonny's naive effervescence being bested week after week by Cher's wisecracks and put downs. To the millions of us watching, they were having great fun. At the very peak of the show's popularity in 1973, Cher walked over to the Los Angeles County Courthouse and put Sonny down one more time. Claiming that he had made her life so miserable that she was suicidal, she decided to end their marriage instead. She moved to Malibu and filed for divorce.

Sonny thought that was a real knife in the back because, after all, he had made Cher a star. He had raised her, taught her everything she knew about show business and molded her into the woman she was.

The childhood of Armenian-American Cher Sarkisian had been an unhappy one, marred by upheaval and strife. Her mother wedded eight times--including three separate marriages to Cher's father. They were poor and Cher spent time in a Los Angeles orphanage while her mother worked nights.

By the time she was 14 years old, problems erupted at home--her mother started clamping down on the wild clothes she wore to school and the wilder boys she wanted to date. Cher rebelled and the two fought bitterly for the next two years. Finally, she couldn't take it anymore and moved out of the house when she turned sixteen.

A girlfriend offered Cher a place to stay and she landed a job at a candy store in Hollywood. When she couldn't pay her rent one month in 1964, Sonny rescued her. He told her he didn't want anything romantic to develop out of it, but that she could live in his house for a while if she did the cooking and cleaning.

She took him up on it, telling her mother that she was moving in with a stewardess and telling Sonny that 19-year-old working girls like her needed a hand like that from time to time. If old Son had only known that he was keeping a 17-year-old high school girl! They kept their distance, though, until one night when Cher had a bad dream. She told Rolling Stone interviewers that she awakened Sonny that night and asked, "Can I get in bed with you?" And he replied: "Yes, but don't bother me."

You see, Sonny had music on his mind just then. He had a dream that he and Cher would some day be renown singers and entertainers. And he had a plan. They teamed up, put an act together and started appearing at nightclubs all over California. Their music caught a wave of enormous popularity and propelled them to stardom with top-10 hit songs like "I Got You Babe" in 1965, "Baby Don't Go" that same year, 1967's "The Beat Goes On," and "All I Ever Need Is You" in 1971.

Throughout the years they were living together and going all over the country singing their hit songs, they told audiences that they were married. They were not. In fact, it wasn't until 1969, shortly before daughter Chastity was born, that they made it legal.

Those Sonny and Cher years play like a kaleidoscope today--sights and sounds we'll never forget. Cher's dazzling and outrageous costumes from which her breasts and bellybutton tried to peak out at us. The repartee. The nose jokes. And little Chastity joining Mom and Dad on the air at the close of each program as they sang "I Got You Babe."

But offstage, Cher was growing restless and increasingly unhappy. She later revealed that in real life Sonny was a "Sicilian dictator husband" who had control of her entire life. She complained that he wouldn't let her play the kind of music she wanted in the house, refused to allow her to play tennis with her friends and actually would ground her in their home. According to Cher, he insisted on approving all movies she attended and forbade her from seeing those he didn't think were right for her. She felt like she was in prison.

Over the course of her marriage to Sonny, Cher simply changed. When they were first together and she was so young, she wanted someone to take care of her. But as she grew older and sought more independence, she wanted him to loosen his grip. Instead, he bullied and bossed her.

She didn't say a word, but frustration with her marriage and emerging hatred for Sonny welled up inside her. It made her sick. She lost her appetite, dropped down to 93 pounds and couldn't sleep well at night. She was miserable. At that point, she decided to take action and finally blurted out to Sonny before a Las Vegas concert that she was going to leave him. It struck him like a bolt out of the blue.

Cher still asks herself why she let Sonny rule her for as long as he did, but she grew determined to have her freedom.

It got vicious.

Court documents reveal that Cher moved out of the couple's million dollar mansion on Carolwood Drive in Los Angeles in November, 1973, and rented a Malibu beach house for $4,000 a month. She took Chastity with her as well as a new live-in boyfriend, music producer David Geffen.

By April, 1974, she wanted back in the Carolwood home, protesting that the Malibu place didn't have enough closets for all her clothes. She figured the mansion was big enough that they could all live there without even bumping into each other. Cher ordered the help to remove all of Sonny's belongings from the master bedroom at Carolwood to make room for her return. Sonny was furious and submitted a bitter testimonial affidavit explaining that Cher was putting the screws to him by refusing to do their TV show anymore or continue their act, and that he couldn't believe that "she now feels she can amicably live under the same roof with me."

Judge Philip Erbsen agreed and in May granted Sonny exclusive occupancy of the home and ordered Cher to stay away. But at 10:00 p.m. on July 8, Cher, David Geffen and her attorney entered the home while Sonny was away and moved all of her clothes and belongings in. They threw Sonny's things out. As Sonny's attorney remembers it, at

10:45 p.m. that night, Cher's attorney telephoned Sonny's at his home and said: "Guess where I'm calling from. I'm calling from Carolwood. Cher is here and she is going to stay here."

His attorney flashed the word to Sonny, who made a frantic phone call to the house. Geffen answered and told him that Cher had taken the home and posted private security guards to keep Sonny out. Then, according to Sonny, Geffen told him: "Go do whatever the f___ you want to do about it." Sonny went through the roof.

The very next day, Sonny marched down to the Los Angeles County Courthouse with his lawyers and demanded an order evicting Cher for her violation of Judge Erbsen's ruling of just two months before. One thing that really rankled him was that Cher had brought David Geffen along to live with her at Carolwood. Sonny claimed in court papers, "I am fearful that Cher's lifestyle with David Geffen has had and will have an extremely detrimental effect on Chastity." On top of that, the way he saw it, Cher and her private army had invaded his home and were occupying it unlawfully.

A new judge fresh to the case, J. L. Weiss, apparently convinced that possession is nine-tenths of the law, refused to order Cher out, however. In a ruling July 10, the judge instead found that Cher was entitled to be there and he ordered Sonny never to go back--even to try to find his clothes. Only Sonny's friends or employees could enter the home on his behalf. Sonny was stunned at how he'd been crunched in the wheels of justice but it soon became clear that the house was one of the least of his worries. Cher was training her sights on his wallet.

In documents filed with the court, she asked that Sonny be ordered to pay her $32,000 a month in temporary alimony, $195,000 so she could buy a condominium in Aspen, Colorado, and $50,000 in temporary attorney fees to pay for the attorneys who helped her break into the home on Carolwood. In her application, Cher revealed that she spent $6,000 a month on new clothes and $2,000 each month on make-up and hairstyling. She wanted Sonny to pay for all of it.

Sonny shot back that Cher didn't need any money from him at all. Court records reveal he protested that if she'd agree to the deal he just made to record a new album, they'd both get one and a half million dollars from the record company the next day. And, he reported that Cher had lost them a mint when she forced CBS to cancel their TV show because she refused to appear on it with him. He thought she had some nerve now to come back and demand that kind of money. He also complained that alimony is not a matter of right but one of necessity and that Cher was not needy by any stretch of the imagination.

Sonny lost this round, too. On July 23, 1974 Judge Goscoe O. Farley ordered him to pay Cher $25,000 a month in temporary alimony for six months, $1,500 a month child support for Chastity and $41,000 to Cher's attorneys for their fees and costs. The only thing that Cher didn't get from the judge was the condo in Aspen.

By this time, it was clear to everyone that the case was so complicated and it involved so much money that it could drag on for years. Both sides agreed that the judge should enter an early order dissolving the marriage and then later decide who should get the money and who should be awarded custody of Chastity. On June 27, 1975, Judge Mario L. Clinco made it official by signing a decree dissolving the marriage of Salvatore P. Bono and Cher Bono.

During the course of their investigation and preparation of this case, Cher's attorneys uncovered a shocking development--in 1972, Cher had actually signed an agreement that Sonny would own her professionally! The papers which she signed created a corporation--Cher Enterprises, Inc. The asset of the corporation was, of course, Cher. Sonny got 95% of the stock in the new company and his attorney took the remaining 5%. An employment contract Cher also signed gave Sonny the right to decide where and when she would work and gave the corporation the right to collect every dime of the money she made performing each year.

It appeared Sonny was going to have the last laugh after all. Cher filed court papers recounting that she asked Sonny to let her out of that contract but that he snorted, "Forget it. I've worked for ten years and if you think I'm going to let you go, just to walk off now, you are crazy."

Sonny started exercising his power. While the divorce proceedings were raging at the courthouse, he negotiated a deal for Cher with MCA Records, telling them that he owned her paper and could make her perform any contract he signed. Cher was livid and asked the judge to void the 1972 employment contract, claiming that Sonny had defrauded her into signing it.

In her testimonial affidavit, she explained that when she and Sonny began their careers together, she was only 17 years old and absolutely inexperienced in business matters. Sonny took care of all the business and when he told her to sign something, she just signed it without reading it. If she ever tried to take time to read it first, Sonny would get mad. She trusted him, so she just signed everything he wanted. She argued that since she didn't know she was signing her life away, the court should refuse to enforce it.

Cher protested that the employment contract meant that she was Sonny's slave and that he owned her, which was illegal since Congress abolished slavery after the Civil War. She swore emphatically, "I do not want Sonny Bono . . . telling me what I can or cannot do" anymore.

Sonny submitted a response saying she had it all wrong. He remembered their original agreement when they were first starting out in show business that they would work together as a two-person act. As he saw it, she went back on that deal when she walked out on him. He tried to convince the judge he wasn't keeping a slave, he was only keeping his enormously successful Sonny and Cher act together.

Judge Clinco didn't buy it; and on July 3, 1979 he issued the final judgment in the case. He threw out the contract Cher had signed and ruled that she was entitled to all the income from her professional performances since the split from Sonny. Cher was also awarded the Carolwood mansion, a 1972 Ferrari and life insurance with a face value of $1,750,000.

To be split 50-50 between them were $300,000 in municipal bonds, the hundreds of thousands of dollars in their checking accounts and all the income which would be earned in the future from records they had made before. It is interesting to note that the judge told Sonny to put $735,000 back into the checking account before it was divided with Cher.

Sonny was given a house on St. Cloud Road in Los Angeles, one in Palm Springs, and a fleet of automobiles including a 1973 Ferrari, 1970 Mercedes, 1975 BMW, 1973 and 1974 Porsches and a 1973 Jaguar.

No permanent alimony was awarded.

Cher was given legal and physical custody of Chastity, but Sonny's visitation time with his little girl was to be equal to the time Cher spent with her. The Judge even ordered Cher to maintain her permanent residence within 100 miles of Los Angeles to make sure Chastity was always close to her dad.

After two years, Geffen was out of the picture and Cher went looking for other entertainment to keep her occupied. The Allman Brothers Band was the most successful of all Southern rock bands at the time and Cher was in the audience enjoying them perform the blues at the Troubadour in Los Angeles in 1975 when a waiter delivered her a note. Lead singer Gregg Allman had seen her recognizable bellybutton winking at him across the room and sent her the note asking to meet her. He came over to her table that night briefly between sets and formally introduced himself. Several weeks later, the rock musician invited her out to dinner at a dark restaurant and what he had for dessert wasn't on the menu. He started sucking each of her fingers. "I don't know this guy, and he sucks my fingers. What the hell is going on?" she remembered thinking at the time for Rolling Stone.

She ran from him that night, but there was something both romantic and dangerous about him that she found strangely appealing. The fingers proved just the beginning and that episode ignited a torrid and lustful four-month courtship. Cher later confided to <u>Glamour</u> that Gregg thought women had two uses--"to make the bed and to make it in the bed." Three days after her divorce from Sonny became official on June 27, 1975, Cher asked Gregg to marry her. A Lear jet quickly whisked them to Nevada for the ceremony and they were husband and wife.

The honeymoon was a short one. Nine days after their wedding, Cher filed for divorce. She admitted that marrying Gregg was "one giant mistake." What prompted her quick reaction was Gregg's heavy drug use. Addicted to heroin, he was an animal to live with. Neither Cher nor Sonny had ever done drugs and she was terrified living with a junkie. In fact, Cher telephoned Gregg in Macon, Georgia, the day she filed to tell him what she'd done, and he was so high he couldn't even comprehend what she was saying. To save their young marriage, Gregg promised to enter a drug rehabilitation center and made a pledge to Cher that he would overcome his drug dependency. She withdrew her divorce petition on July 30, 1975, after one of Gregg's doctors assured her Gregg was serious about rehabilitation.

And, for a few weeks, Gregg stayed clean; but he started taking drugs again when his band hit the road for a four-month concert tour. By that time an added complication developed for Cher--she was pregnant. She would have to try to keep the marriage afloat.

On July 10, 1976, a healthy baby boy was born-- blonde, blue-eyed Elijah Blue Allman. Cher and Gregg were proud and happy, but their days together were numbered.

It is now obvious that there were two forces at work in the marriage, each pulling on Cher. First, there was her raw physical attraction to him. By all accounts, he was a love machine. Cher explained to <u>Rolling Stone</u> that their lovemaking was like the song lyric, "too hot not to cool down." She continued, "our loving was incredibly passionate." She has said she never really loved any other man the way she loved him. In the bedroom, they were intense and red hot.

But there was nothing to back it up in the rest of the house; and that was the other force pressuring her.

She would admit in candid moments that Gregg was not too smart. But who demands IQ tests when they're ripping the other's clothes off? No, what finally outweighed the good times was Cher's anguish as her husband self-destructed on drugs and alcohol in front of her eyes.

Because of her zest for life, she is adamant in her opposition to drugs. It's her opinion that both drugs and alcohol ruin a person's body; and those beliefs conflicted every day with Gregg's alcohol and drug abuse. Throughout their three-year marriage, Gregg was unsuccessful in fighting his addictions. He was in and out of institutions and rehab programs. Within his reach was the promise of the good life with Cher and Elijah, but he couldn't be changed. Cher was drained and simply couldn't live with it anymore. She filed for legal separation in 1977 and later for an outright divorce. This time, she made it stick.

With Gregg out of her life, she devoted her considerable energy and talent to becoming one of the top movie stars in Hollywood. Outstanding performances in *Silkwood*, *Mask*, *Suspect* and *The Witches of Eastwick* established her as a serious and professionally respected actress. Her role in *Moonstruck* earned her the 1988 Academy Award for Best Actress.

But Cher is an enigma--she works her ass off but she also hangs it out. She is the consummate hard working professional performer who not only gives a thousand percent to every role, song and appearance but who lifts weights and trains exhaustively two hours a day to stay trim and healthy. At the same time, she's a rebel who dresses outrageously to show more skin than she conceals and who shocks people with foul-mouthed language more identified with street gangs than petite starlets.

She showed a national television audience those two sides of her in an appearance with Sonny on a 1987 David Letterman program. Nostalgically reuniting with Sonny after ten years and after having called him a "pig" as a husband, the two of them sang "I Got You Babe" in an emotional denouement. Yet, for that misty-eyed occasion, she wore black knee-high boots with nothing much more than garters and lace from the boots to her skimpy top. Literally, without any pants or dress to cover herself, her ass was hanging out and, by the way, revealed a large gluteous tatoo which prompted an inquiry about her posterior from Letterman. Cher is indeed a free spirit.

She defies convention in another way--by dating boys in their twenties fresh from the high school prom. She has dated Tom Cruise, Val Kilmer, Rupert Everett--all in their twenties, assorted young musicians and one hockey hunk. Currently, the 42-year-old actress is having a steamy live-in affair with 24-year-old Rob Camilletti, a male model and former bagel baker who, dressed in skin-tight pants and with looks to kill, Cher met at a New York nightclub on her 40th birthday.

Their relationship is very serious and, in fact, Rob is the one who kisses and entwines with Cher in the lustful video version of her hot "I Found Someone" record. Later in 1988, however, it appeared to some that Cher had landed a Sean Penn when Rob was arrested outside her Los Angeles home for assaulting a tabloid photographer with Cher's $87,000 Ferrari. Rob says the wheels accidentally locked, the stunned photographer says the guy rammed him with the car, and the cops said it would cost Cher $2,000 to spring him from the slammer. She paid it and Rob went on to strut his stuff in a small role in the new film *Loverboy*.

But Rob and the other young men she's been with have made Cher happy. So why should anyone else care? She enjoys herself, has a good time with them and lives life to the limit. Everyone deserves that.

Chastity is now 20 years old and Elijah is 13. Home is an Egyptian-style mansion on Benedict Canyon Drive in Beverly Hills and an elegant condo in Greenwich Village. Sonny lives in Palm Springs where he owns a restaurant. April, 1988, was a big month for Sonny--he was elected Mayor of Palm Springs and his young wife Mary gave birth to a bouncing baby boy Bono. On New Year's Eve, 1988, Sonny opened the Palm Springs Convention Center with a new act--Sonny and daughter Chas teamed up to sing beautifully to the delight of everyone in the audience.

Gregg, who moved back to Macon, Georgia, is another story. He has essentially dropped out of Cher's life and his son's life, too, seeing Elijah only rarely. In 1979, Cher wrote a song about Gregg which she entitled "My Song," and which she sang in concerts across the country. The lyrics lament that Gregg was "too far gone, he doesn't want to know me, he'll never get to know his son."

Obviously, the road hasn't always been easy for Cher. Her two very public divorces took an enormous emotional toll. She admitted that she was so depressed after breaking up with Gregg that she hated her life. She now criticizes herself for choosing wrong husbands and considers both marriages as "disasters."

As she looks back, she figures divorce is a part of growing up today. Too, she consoles herself with the realization that two wonderful children were born of those marriages.

How did she cope with her divorces? She has told friends that her greatest strength is that she refuses to give up. And it shows.

Farrah Fawcett at the National Conference of Christians
and Jews' 24th Annual Humanitarian Awards Dinner at the
Beverly Hilton Hotal to honor Producer Leonard Goldberg.
(Janet Gough, Celebrity Photo)

Chapter 4

Farrah Fawcett

Farrah Fawcett was not an ugly child. By the time she was in high school, her thick blonde hair cascaded around a stunning face. She had a picture perfect complexion and a dazzling smile. Shapely and slender, she was a knock-out. Can you imagine someone that glamorous in your high school algebra class, floating down the hallway between home room and social studies? That's why she was voted best looking girl in her Corpus Christi high school for three years in a row.

As a freshman at the University of Texas in 1965, she was voted one of the ten most beautiful girls on that campus out of 12,000 coeds. At her sorority's first party of the school year, she got so many dates that she was booked up through February. By March, she was going steady with the big man on campus--quarterback Greg Lott of the Longhorn's football team.

She was so attached to her football hero that she rejected numerous offers of modeling jobs in California. But when Greg fumbled Farrah in the summer between her junior and senior years by telling her he wanted to date other girls, she bolted straight for Hollywood.

She was a bright-eyed 21-year-old when she arrived in Tinsel Town in July of 1968. Within two weeks, 29-year-old Lee Majors, one of Hollywood's most eligible bachelors, picked Farrah's photograph out of a stack of 8 x 10 glossy prints in his agent's office. Lee, already an established TV star riding high in the popular *Big Valley* series as Barbara Stanwyck's stepson Heath, apparently hadn't seen anything quite as lovely in some time on the Barkley ranch.

He called her up for a date, she nervously accepted, and they went to a Jim Weatherly concert on July 28, 1968. Lee was so stunned by Farrah's breathtaking radiance in person that he didn't say a word for ten minutes as he drove to the concert. He was absolutely tongue-tied. When he finally did speak, he stammered that she was the most beautiful person he'd ever seen in his entire life.

Not an ineffective line to use on a first date, even if Farrah had to wait ten minutes for it. It worked. They went out again the next night and the night after that. It was dating Hollywood style--he'd pick her up in his limousine and take her to famous, star-packed restaurants or to the set of the *Big Valley* where she would watch him film his show. Her eyes grew bigger. A short time later, she moved into his Malibu beach home where they lived together for five years before getting married.

During those early years together, Farrah was happy playing tennis, cooking Lee's meals and oil painting. Neighbors found her down-to-earth, genuine and unpretentious. Lee idolized her.

When Farrah told him she was ready to launch her own career, he took charge of it and taught her the business. He booked guest appearances for her on his *Owen Marshall* and *Six Million Dollar Man* shows and went studio-to-studio trying to persuade executives to sign Farrah to a contract.

At first, the only contract she signed was one with him. On July 28, 1973--exactly five years to the day after they met--they were married in a traditional ceremony at the Bel Air Hotel. Farrah's father, owner of a Houston janitorial service, gave her away and her older sister was matron of honor. Lee's parents, brother, and son by his former marriage, Lee, Jr., were all in attendance. Lee and Farrah didn't want a celebrity, Hollywood-type wedding and they kept it a quiet family affair.

Now known as Farrah Fawcett-Majors, her star began to rise. She made a big splash in TV commercials as she licked Ultra Brite toothpaste from her dentally perfect teeth, spread Noxzema skin cream on her pretty tanned face and blow dried the Wella Balsam out of her mane of golden hair. She sold Fabrege perfumes and Mercury Cougars. Millions began to notice those sultry commercials and compare her to screen siren Marilyn Monroe.

And then she got the big break which jetisoned her career into true stardom--the role as Jill Monroe in *Charlie's Angels*, a new ABC series set to premier in 1976. She was only 29. *Angels* became the most popular new TV show in

America in just a few weeks as Farrah, Kate Jackson (as Sabrina) and Jaclyn Smith (as Kelly) made Wednesday nights their own.

The comely girls portrayed private detectives who usually worked undercover to solve cases assigned to them over the telephone by the unseen Charlie. Often, the trail would lead to such places as health spas or beaches where, alas, they would have to squeeze into their skin-tight bikinis or halter-tops and short shorts. Even when they were "fully" dressed on the show, the bra salesman never made a dime because it was like ABC had posted a "no bras allowed" sign on the set. Weekly, the girls jiggled after bad guys until the tongue of every red-blooded male viewer in the country lapped out of his mouth. Feminists gagged, protesting that the show was sexually exploitative and chauvinistic. Those criticisms, of course, only drew several million more men closer to their TV sets each Wednesday.

Sabrina was the smart one, Kelly the streetwise one and Jill the blonde athletic one. Charlie was the dumb one because he never came by to check out those popping bikinis.

Farrah was an overnight sensation--the nation's newest sex symbol. A revealing poster of her in a wet swim suit sold more than eight million copies and her stunning face appeared on 116 different magazine covers. Playboy reported that she was the symbol of a shift in America's perception of what was sexy in the 70's. . . from Farrah on, being healthy and athletic was erotic.

At home, Lee was the boss. He wore the pants and Farrah baked the brownies. Even though *Angels* filmed 12 hours a day, Lee insisted that her contract contain a clause that she could leave the studio early enough every night to get home and cook his dinner.

At the end of her series' first spectacular season, Farrah left the show to pursue a movie career. But she got off to an embarrassing start, bombing in the forgettable *Someone Killed Her Husband* (the joke around Hollywood was that the film should have been named *Someone Killed Her Ca-*

reer), *Sunburn* and *Saturn Three*. Each one made Charlie on the speakerphone look like Academy Award material.

At age 32, her career was suddenly on the skids and she decided to do some spring housecleaning. She fired her manager. She fired her lawyer. And she fired Lee. She announced a trial separation in the fall of 1979, explaining that she was a different person than the innocent starlet he married six years before. She had grown up. While Farrah readily acknowledged that she owed her show business success to Lee, it was clear she wasn't happy with their marriage and the control he exerted over her. Instead, she began thinking about what she wanted for herself rather than what Lee told her she should do. She also grew noticeably less deferential to him. America's pin-up girl was becoming a liberated woman.

To his friends, Lee began opening up about what it was like being married to such a beautiful woman--it was exactly what most men fantasize about, walking into a room with her and having everyone stare in envy. And he missed it. To win her back, he cut a record album of love songs which he publicly dedicated to her. During the first few months of their separation, they talked every day on the telephone and Lee firmly believed that they would weather the storm and get back together.

Lee was so concerned about Farrah being alone in Los Angeles that he asked one of his old carousing bachelor buddies, Ryan O'Neal, to look in on her during his next trip to L.A. It turned out that was like dispatching a hungry fox to guard the chickens. Lee telephoned a few days later to see how things were and he was flabbergasted when Ryan told him he had fallen in love with Farrah. He just couldn't believe Ryan would stab him in the back.

With Farrah and Ryan together, Lee filed for divorce in May, 1980. He was 41 and Farrah was 32. Since there were no children to fight over, the only issue was how their property was going to be divided. Lee wouldn't let her have his $2.5 million Bel Air mansion, arguing that he had bought it with his TV income long before he married Farrah. He forced a four-day trial in which Judge Harry Schafer painstakingly divided up the property, except for the house. The Judge said he wouldn't decide who would get the house until he went out and saw it himself.

On the last day of the trial, Lee and Farrah had dinner together alone at a quiet restaurant. After tenderly reminiscing about all the good times they had together and all the happy years, Lee gave her the house. He told the New York Times afterward, "She's a nice lady, and I still love her very much." He played the gentleman right to the end.

The Judge signed the divorce decree, lamenting that it had been a "splitting headache" of a case. Farrah was free.

She reveled in being independent for the first time in her life. Looking back on the relationship with Lee which began when she was only a 21-year-old college girl, she figured he'd never given her the chance to be her own person. She felt she'd been denied the time to find out who she was and what made her happy because she was expected to spend her time making Lee happy. She even remembered worrying about what she was going to fix Lee for dinner in the middle of scenes she was shooting for *Charlie's Angels*.

But after her divorce, she is finally in control of her own life. Nobody tells her what to do.

Her show business decisions appear to have been wise ones and her career is back on the fast track. A starring role in the hit movie *Cannonball Run* re-established her; her superlative performances in the made-for-TV movies *Murder in Texas*, *Nazi Hunter*, and *The Burning Bed* earned her wide critical acclaim; and her films *Extremities* and *Poor Little Rich Girl* confirmed her as a heavyweight among dramatic actresses.

For her private life, she decided to live with Ryan O'Neal, sharing homes in Malibu Beach and Bel Air. They're both fitness fanatics and jog every morning together on the beach.

Farrah's typical day includes a morning workout, some racquetball and a sauna, a lunch of raisins and nuts, an afternoon reading scripts and tending to business, and an evening of tennis. She likes to feed Ryan a home-cooked dinner with homemade ice cream. Her specialties are broiled chicken and veal.

After living together for five years, they decided to have a baby; and in February of 1985 Farrah gave birth to a seven-pound son at a natural childbirth clinic in L.A. They named him Redmond, after the character Ryan played in the movie *Barry Lyndon*. The baby's full name is Redmond James Fawcett O'Neal.

The tabloids have had a field day since Redmond's birth, reporting that Ryan has been pressuring Farrah to marry him and stay home to raise the baby "just like normal people do." He is described as shocked that Farrah has continued her career at full speed and left Redmond to be cared for by sitters and nannies. The gossip sheets blare that Farrah goes crazy and starts screaming every time Ryan brings up the idea of marriage.

Ryan is very self-conscious about it. The tabloids tattled that a drunk swaggered up to them at a restaurant one night and demanded to know when they were going to get married. Ryan, flushed with anger, threw a forkful of spaghetti right in the guy's face.

According to reports, Farrah and Ryan have had loud fights about marriage and she rages that he's not going to force her to lead a Betty Crocker existence. Farrah apparently sees her refusal to be pressured into a formal marriage as a sign of the freedom and independence she has fought for in her life. Two different tabloids informed their readers that one fight in June, 1985 was so raucous that neighbors called the security patrol. It was during that ugly blowup that Farrah kicked Ryan out of the Bel Air mansion.

Within a few days, though, they had patched things up and were back together. Their peace pact reportedly was that Ryan would control his notorious temper and stop badgering her to marry him.

Three years later, false alarms sounded on the wedding watch when Hollywood insiders flashed the word that Farrah had finally given in and agreed to a June 18, 1988 Paris wedding. But as that date came and went, it was clearer than ever that Farrah's slavery to Lee Majors had been so repulsive to her and her divorce from him so painful that she was going to resist ever marrying again.

Wives and husbands often change over time into persons who are quite different from who they married. Ask Lee Majors, who married a deferential, traditional, supportive young wife from Texas. Ask the feminists who so vehemently criticized *Charlies Angels* for chauvinistically pandering to men.

Just listen to Farrah Fawcett today. How has her life improved since she divorced Lee Majors? "I don't like to take sh-- from anybody, my lover, my parents, my friends. I don't want anybody telling me what to think or what to do," she told TV Guide.

The picture of independence. Like a phoenix rising from the ashes of her divorce, she flies free as a bird.

Nationally syndicated advice columnist Ann Landers.
(Photo: the Chicago Tribune)

Chapter 5

Ann Landers

Each day, 85 million of us read the peppery syndicated advice column of Ann Landers in our hometown newspapers. People with troubled marriages or other family problems have turned to Ann for help since 1955, when her first brisk column appeared in the Chicago Sun-Times. Her real name is Esther "Eppie" Lederer; Ann Landers is the name used by the Sun-Times' advice columnist she replaced in the Fifties.

She's known for her often sharp and biting responses. To a man who once wrote in complaining of his girlfriend's odd hobby of keeping an apartment full of canaries and parrots, Ann replied: "Your lady friend is strictly for the birds. The love-nest is much too crowded. Take off."

But once married, that was a different story. For decades, Ann wrote that under no circumstances should people get divorced. Her reasoning was that when you marry, you make a commitment and simply stick with it. Even if the marriage turned out be lousy, she advised making the best of it--especially if there were children.

Her husband of 36 years, Jules Lederer, must not have read all those columns because over dinner in Chicago one night in 1974 he told Ann he had been having an affair with a 28-year old nurse whom he'd met at his doctor's office in London. He had been keeping her, ironically, in the house in England that he and Ann had bought as a second home.

Ann's reaction that night was total shock. "I had absolutely no idea," she was quoted by the Associated Press as saying, "That was quite a bomb for him to drop between the soup and salad."

Jolted, Ann was embarrassed because no one in her family had ever been divorced. In fact, when she was growing up, she couldn't remember even knowing anybody who was divorced.

It had been a storybook wedding in 1939, 36 years before. Ann and her twin sister, Abigail Van Buren (whose
real name is Pauline "Popo" Phillips) were married in an
extravagant double ring ceremony at Shaare-Zion Syna-
gogue in Sioux City, Iowa. The twins had grown up in
Sioux City, where their father was a wealthy movie theater
operator.

Two days shy of their 21st birthday, Ann and Abby
walked down the aisle as 750 guests marveled at the ele-
gance around them. There were three rabbis officiating,
twenty-two attendants and several mounted police outside
to keep order.

The brides wore identical satin gowns which sparkled
amid the opulence. Several hundred townspeople who
hadn't even been invited gathered outside just to watch. It
was truly a grand and magnificent ceremony.

That night, the four newlyweds climbed on the east-
bound train for Chicago--and went on their honeymoons together to the Edgewater Beach Hotel on Lake Michigan.

After that, though, the twins went their separate ways.
Abby's husband quickly became hugely successful in business as the owner of the Presto appliance company . They
settled comfortably in Beverly Hills. Ann's husband was a
slow starter by comparison and moved his family around
the midwest eight times in the first seven years of their marriage, going from job to job. But by the end of their first year
of marriage, Ann and Jules found real happiness in the birth
of their baby daughter, Margo.

While Ann would pride herself on making do with whatever Jules earned from his rather low-paying jobs, he
showed some real genius in 1958 that would make them
millionaires. He founded Budget Rent-a-Car as an alterna-
tive to high priced car rental companies. Starting from
scratch with a one-lot "fleet" of used cars, he built Budget
into a $500 million dollar corporation with outlets around
the world. The idea of cheaper rental cars caught on with
the public and Jules made a mint.

The wives were busy, too. Ann spent the first 17 years
of her marriage as a housewife raising young Margo and

donating much of her free time to her favorite political and charitable campaigns. She was even the local Democratic county chairman when they lived in Eau Claire, Wisconsin, and was in line to be named to the Democratic National Committee before Jules moved her one last time . . . to Chicago in 1955.

When Ann and Jules relocated in Chicago, Ann entered a contest sponsored by the <u>Sun-Times</u> to find a replacement for their advice columnist, Ann Landers, who had died that summer. Eppie won, her first column appeared on October 16, 1955 and the rest is an avalanche of advice to increasing millions of readers.

At the same time out on the West coast, sister Abby's pen was restless and three months after Ann debuted her <u>Sun-Times</u> column, Abby premiered as advice columnist "Dear Abby" in the <u>San Francisco Chronicle</u> and <u>New York Daily Mirror</u>.

It was to Abby that Ann first reached out for help in 1974 on the night Jules told her there was another woman. Ann called her from Chicago and whispered "Come, Pussy, I need you very much." Abby caught the next plane. When she arrived, Ann's eyes were burning red from hours of crying.

Abby later looked back on the marriage and put it into her own perspective. She felt Ann really lost Jules years before when she got so busy with her work that Jules had lots of time on his hands. He spent it in London where he met that nurse. And, being married to a celebrity was difficult for Jules. He just got tired of being Mr. Ann Landers. As Abby saw it, it wasn't really that much of a shock when Ann's marriage fell apart.

Maybe not to Abby, but Ann was flabbergasted. And she was hurting deeply. Ann's friends rallied around her. Father Theodore Hesburgh, the President of Notre Dame University, spent five comforting hours with her and emphasized that she had not failed, that it wasn't anyone's fault and that she must not torture herself by looking back and asking where she went wrong. He told her to look forward and move on with her life.

Walter and Betsy Cronkite, Barbara Walters and Art Buchwald invited her to their homes on the East coast to spend time away from Chicago.

Ann, outwardly at least, began to snap out of her depression quickly. She had advised hundreds of readers over the years who faced tough times to "Kwitcher bellyachin' buttercup" and she would put it to use in her own moment of need. Daughter Margo, who called her dad an alleycat for what he'd done, counted that her mother had only three bad days as she adjusted and accepted the failure of her marriage.

The irony of a divorce falling on America's best-known advice columnist was not lost on Ann. Although she believed what happened to her was beyond her control, she feared editors and readers across the country would scoff at her for not being able to manage her own life while appearing in hundreds of newspapers as the nation's problem solver. She thought it might end her career as Ann Landers.

She decided to tell the world of her nightmare. The Ann Landers column of July 1, 1975, broke the news to stunned millions. In it, she said flat out that she and Jules were divorcing. She confided that as she wrote those words it was like she was referring to a letter from one of her readers and that it seemed "unreal" that she was writing about her own marriage.

Ann took the high ground and called Jules loving and generous. She said she'd always cherish the years they were together. The marriage had been a good one.

Why didn't it last forever? "The lady with all the answers does not know the answer to this one," she admitted. But she saw a lesson for others--don't say it can't happen to you.

With those few sentences she concluded what she described as both the most difficult and shortest column she'd ever written. Ann then asked the editors of the hundreds of papers who were running it to leave the rest of her column space blank "as a memorial to one of the world's best marriages that didn't make it to the finish line."

Thirty thousand readers across the country rallied to her side, writing letters of support. They wrote to comfort her and to insist that she continue to write the column. No newspaper dropped her because of her divorce and many actually ran editorials expressing their compassion for her and their continued confidence in her.

Ann was pulling herself up. She knew how to cope with crisis. Her own formula for dealing with trouble was to accept it as inevitable in every life, look it square in the eye, hold your head high and not let it defeat you. She practiced what she had preached and repeated to herself those words which gave her special comfort: "this too will pass in time."

Ann philosophized that we can't control what others do to us or prevent them from doing us wrong. But we can control our own reaction to it. What she did was to refuse to be consumed with hate and bitterness. Hatred, she reasoned, was like an acid and it can do more damage to the container it's stored in than to the object on which it's poured.

For 36 years, Ann had bought Jules' clothes and looked after him. Even after he moved out of their posh Lake Shore Drive apartment, she sent him dozens of new shirts, boxer shorts and socks. She had soup delivered in case he caught a cold. She was worried about him living alone and made him promise to remarry as soon as their divorce was final.

Ann had filed for divorce on October 9, 1975 in Cook County Circuit Court alleging that Jules had violated his marriage vows and engaged in "extreme and repeated acts of mental cruelty" which caused Ann "embarrassment, humiliation and anguish."

In his formal answer to Ann's petition, Jules denied that the couple split because of any intolerable conduct on his part. Further, he charged that it was Ann who hadn't "always conducted herself as a true, kind and affectionate wife."

Later, in a discreet fifteen minute hearing in the chambers of Judge Hyman Feldman, Ann and Margo testified about the break-up. Jules didn't attend, but was represented by his attorney. The Judge found that the evidence established that Jules had indeed been violating his marriage vows for three years. He signed an order formally dissolving the marriage and returning the parties to the status of single persons.

Within a week, Jules married his English girlfriend, Elizabeth, whom he described as glamorous, attractive and intelligent.

Ann went on with her own life. Margo even sensed that her mother's divorce had added a new dimension to Ann's responses to readers' letters by mellowing her. Ann found that all the time she used to spend buying Jules' shorts was now time that she had for herself.

Her transition from being married to being single was a smooth one. Four years later, she told the Associated Press that she would like to remarry sometime and described her idea of a perfect mate as a nondrinker and nonsmoker who was successful and would not be overwhelmed by her success. She thought a top doctor or lawyer in his fifties would fill the bill as long as she was sexually aroused by him.

Born July 4, 1918 and now in her seventies, the 5' 2", 110 pound Ann keeps eight secretaries busy opening her mail. She works 10 to 12 hours every day seven days a week, dispensing advice on every conceivable topic. And she doesn't hesitate to lash a reader with the old wet noodle when they need it because she always calls 'em like she sees 'em.

Her column still has zip. She ignited a nationwide giggle early in 1985 when she published the results of a survey of 90,000 women readers which showed 70% of them preferred hugging to sexual intercourse. Men threw down their lunch boxes and shook their heads.

In another 1985 column, she explained what 30 years of writing Ann Landers had meant to her. It was "an opportunity to educate, to shine a spotlight on ignorance and fear, to comfort the afflicted and afflict the comfortable." And she reveled in all of it.

Ann was on top of the world, her column seen every day by the largest reading audience on earth. In a burst of spunk, she walked out on her boss at the <u>Sun-Times</u> in 1987 and set up new offices at the rival <u>Chicago Tribune</u>, taking with her the 1100 newspapers that syndicated her column. As it had done thirty-two years before, the <u>Sun-Times</u> ran a contest to find a replacement and eventually tabbed a young male reporter for the <u>Wall Street Journal</u> and a 47-year-old woman lawyer from Massachusetts to write that paper's new advice column. They'll be eating Ann's dust for a long time.

In personal appearances the last ten years, Ann has readily acknowledged that her divorce was the "major tragedy" of her life. At the same time, she quotes ancient philosophers who taught that no one can touch the stars unless they've been in the depths of despair and fought their way back.

We're glad you're back, Ann.

Lorenzo Lamas, star of "Falcon Crest" at the Nosotros Awards Dinner at the Beverly Hilton Hotel. (Scott Downie, Celebrity Photo)

Chapter 6

Lorenzo Lamas

Lorenzo Lamas burst onto the national scene in a lurid 1979 <u>People</u> magazine photograph slipping out of his wet swim trunks at a secluded Southern California beach. His nearly naked body revealed a broad, muscular chest thatched with a bountiful crop of manly hair which glistened in the sun. Cheesecake met beefcake in that photograph and a new Hollywood sex symbol was crowned.

Lorenzo is Fernando Lamas' strapping son and, after all, he should look "mahvelous." When he was taking his clothes off for <u>People</u>, he was 21 years old; and ever since he has reigned as Hollywood's most virile and notorious Latin lover. His sexual appetite seems insatiable. Young Lorenzo's first marriage lasted ten months and cost him $3,200 a month in alimony. His second marriage rolled along for 18 months, produced two children and collapsed into one of the most vile child custody battles ever fought out in Los Angeles County Superior Court. Since then, he's been playing the field and the female cast members of *Falcon Crest*.

The M.O. never seems to vary--he loves 'em and leaves 'em.

Lorenzo spent 21 years getting his body ready for those <u>People</u> photographers. He was raised by his stepmother, legendary swimming champion Esther Williams, and learned to swim before he could walk. A human outboard motor in the water, he was on the swim team in both high school and college. He also played football in school, wrestled and broke the school's discus record. Lifting weights topped off his work outs every day.

The finished product after all those years was a beefy, brawny 6'2", 185-pound musclehead. But he was also tall, dark, handsome and suave--packaging one can't acquire in the weight room. To be sure, Lorenzo got his in the delivery room 21 years before.

The son of glamorous movie stars Fernando Lamas and Arlene Dahl, who divorced when he was two, the boy was a chip off the paternal block. Fernando was the big screen's all-time Latin lover, type cast throughout his career as a handsome, romantic and debonair lady killer. Today's generation, as well, can relate to the Fernando mystique thanks to comedian Billy Crystal's popular Nando impersonation. The Nando philosophy was that it's more important to look good than feel good and, as Fernando himself would coo to screen conquests, "darling you look mahvelous."

Off the movie lots, too, Fernando was a seductive swashbuckler in his private life, romping through four marriages and a gossip column trail of other romantic interludes. He would leave this legacy of libido to his son.

Lorenzo idolized his dad and spent every minute he could with him. Little wonder, then, that so much of Nando rubbed off on the boy. And when little Lorenzo shot up to be 6'2" big Lorenzo, he was ready to take on Hollywood with both the bulges and the rakishness that are his trademarks today.

Despite his big name celebrity parents, Lorenzo charted his own humble route into show business. Wanting to make it on his own, he enrolled at Santa Monica Junior College to take acting classes. He worked his own way through school with part-time jobs at McDonald's frying hamburgers and as a weightlifting instructor at Jack LaLanne's health spa.

His first break in the movies came when he was chosen to play Olivia Newton-John's handsome high school jock boyfriend in *Grease*. After that he landed the part that made him an overnight TV celebrity--playing Lance Cumson on ABC's *Falcon Crest*. Since it premiered in 1981, that nighttime soap opera has chronicled the sordid affairs of a California wine-making dynasty ruled by conniving matriarch Angela Channing (Jane Wyman). Angela is the wealthiest and most powerful wine baroness in the area and Lance is her spoiled prodigal grandson. Sinister and diabolical, Lance eagerly does his grandmother's dirty work as she schemes for money and tries to control the lives of everyone around her.

The storylines typically have Lance putting in a hard day's work being evil and rotten, then spending the evening seducing any one of a number of females who are hanging on around the estate. On-camera trysts with Apollonia, Ana Alicia and Robin Greer have been running subplots of the program for years and allow Lorenzo the opportunity to do something with his trademark sensuality other than count bottles in the wine cellar.

What became clear about Lorenzo from his first weeks on *Falcon Crest* was that he was a free spirit. His antidote for the glare of Hollywood's lights was to buy a Harley-Davidson and spend his entire summer vacation riding the California highways with other bikers. His answer to the conformity and sanitization demanded by the network and *Falcon Crest* producers was to have three huge tattoos-- one of a motorcycle, one of a woman riding a horse and one of a tiger--burned onto his arms and back. And his way of dealing with his lust was to sow plenty of wild oats.

On October 1, 1981 Lorenzo married Victoria Hilbert, a stunning woman 12 years his senior. While his new TV show survived the crucial first season on the air, the marriage didn't and they separated ten months after the wedding. No big deal. Lorenzo told reporters: "She was just the wrong person at the wrong time. The same voice that told me to marry her told me to move on." But he paid for his freedom, as revealed in the court file's marital settlement agreement approved by Judge Jacqueline L. Weiss. On every Wednesday for 16 months he would pay his ex $750 to call the whole thing off. On top of that, he had to pay her $2,500 a month for six months to cover her living expenses as she adjusted to the single life again. Then, he was ordered to pay Victoria's monthly telephone bill as long as it didn't exceed $100 and to purchase a van for her. And away she drove out of his life.

Back in mach speed circulation, Lorenzo vowed never to get tied down again; but within just a few months he met publicist Michele Smith in New York and they married on

May 22, 1983. On December 19, 1983, son Alvaro Joshua ("A.J." to his parents) was born, and they started to live the idyllic, cozy family life of Ward and June Cleaver. Michele knew what Lorenzo expected of her. "Being a Latin, it's very important to me that when I come home from work she has dinner on the table and a beer ready for me," he told interviewers for Cosmopolitan.

Lorenzo the Domesticated came to believe that fatherhood was great and he took the responsibilities of being a dad very seriously. To prove it, he gave up the Hollywood party scene for warm slippers and Fisher-Price toys. A big night at the Lamas house was Mom and Dad staying up to watch Johnny Carson and eating chocolate chip ice cream.

It was suburban bliss. The lovebirds even made a video together (*The Joy of Natural Childbirth*, MCA Home Video, $39.95) in which they explained and demonstrated the Lamaze method of natural childbirth. Against the background patter of little feet, Michele got pregnant again and Lorenzo gloated to all his friends that she was "the perfect wife."

It lasted 18 months and then burst like a cheap condom. Things got so bad that they both filed for divorce, apparently leaving nothing to chance, and they didn't even wait until Michele gave birth to their second child. On February 20, 1985 Lorenzo moved out and took a room at the Hollywood Hotel on Sunset Boulevard. Then the fireworks began. What ensued was the messiest child custody battle waged in Hollywood in years.

Lorenzo fought hard for custody of A.J. He complained that because Michele was more of a zombified party animal than a mother, she wasn't providing the little boy with proper care.

Aura Mendoza, the matronly lady hired as A.J.'s nanny, then came forward to tell it all. She confirmed that Michele and her wild friends would party loudly all night behind the locked doors of her bedroom, that Michele would often fall dead asleep on the floor all day and that little A.J. would roam loose in the house in dirty diapers while Michele was out cold.

Grandmother Esther Williams couldn't take it anymore and she offered to assume custody of A.J. and care for him during the day while Lorenzo was filming *Falcon Crest.*

The Judge acted swiftly and sternly. Michele was awarded temporary custody of A.J. but Nanny Mendoza was ordered to provide the child's daily care. The Judge even issued a ruling restraining Michele from harassing Mrs. Mendoza or interfering with her work.

Lorenzo was granted visitation including alternating weekends and some days during the week. If he was out of town on location, Esther Williams was allowed to exercise those rights.

By the end of 1985, things cooled down to the point that Lorenzo and Michele started working things out. He told reporters that Michele was "going to go on with her life, and I'm going to go on with my life, and we'll share the boy." They agreed to divorce terms and joint custody of A.J. Lorenzo apologized to Michele for "overreacting" earlier in the year by fighting for custody and dragging her name through the mud. They both pledged a good relationship for the sake of their son.

Michele gave birth to the baby girl she'd been carrying in November, 1985--the same month their divorce was final. They named her Shayne.

After being confined in that marriage for 18 months and winning his freedom, he ran with it like a wild mustang. Nothing seemed too dangerous or daring. Turned on by high speed auto racing, he took up the sport and nearly killed himself a few months later when he lost control and rammed his car into a concrete wall at 110 miles an hour at the Riverside International Raceway.

For the 11th Annual Circus of the Stars in 1986, he walked barechested into a cage of 11 tigers and commanded them to do a variety of tricks. One of the angry 500-pound beasts bit him on the wrist. He miraculously escaped injury.

But when it came to the eligible starlets in town, Lorenzo was the animal. He prowled as a pleasure seeking hedonistic stallion. It got so bad that one of his buddies was quoted by gossip columnists as saying, "When Lorenzo sees a pretty girl, his head snaps so fast he gets whiplash." He went through a whole bevy of Hollywood's most gorgeous and shapely knock-outs, including Lydia Cornell of *Too Close for Comfort*, movie actress Jennifer O'Neill and *Falcon Crest* vamps Apollonia and Ana Alicia. Of course, there were many more young starlets who were not yet household names, but who made it in Lorenzo's house. One 17-year-old particularly tickled his fancy. His dating and bedding habits are voracious and friends say he dates more than one woman at the same time.

The *Falcon Crest* set has always worked like a singles bar for Lorenzo and by 1987 he had picked up another girlfriend there. Ironically, it was shapely young actress Robin Greer, who played Dina, his lover on the show. The writers frequently had them cavorting in bed together on the program, but it was off screen that their relationship really sizzled. Spending their working days in bed just got them primed for jumping right back into the sack when they got home. Living together for a while in a Spanish-style home in Malibu, they even publicly talked marriage as they romped.

But the Malibu bedsprings went still when Lorenzo started chasing yet another new *Falcon Crest* lovely--22-year-old Daphne Ashbrook, who joined the cast in 1988. Robin was out, Daphne was in and the mating dance perfected by the stud Lorenzo began afresh.

Daphne moved in with him, got pregnant and gave birth to a baby girl in September, 1988. Soon, it was announced they'd marry on December 18th. But a month before the wedding, Lorenzo left Daphne and his publicist confirmed that the couple had agreed to split up. By January, he turned around and quickly married shapely Kathleen Kinmont, a young actress who is the daughter of his former *Falcon Crest* co-star, Abby Dalton.

Some would criticize that Lorenzo seems to enjoy the conquest, but when it comes to changing the diapers, he bolts. But there are dynamics involved in these personal relationships which are unobservable to outsiders and which might well justify his actions. Ex-wife Michele doesn't think so. To her he's just a heel.

Within days of the birth of Lorenzo's new daughter by his live-in girlfriend, Michele smacked him with a stinging lawsuit claiming he had been ignoring his other two children. In her biting complaint filed in Los Angeles in October, Michele charged that "Lorenzo has not spent more than just a couple of week-ends with Shayne in the last two and one-half years" and that he had only "spent minimal time" with A.J. She alleged that in response to her pleas that he spend more time with his kids, he told her he was too busy and that they "were not a priority."

Michele contended in the lawsuit that Lorenzo had been dodging his parental responsibilities to help care for the children. It was also her belief that his neglect had caused the children emotional harm. Specifically, she stated that A.J. and Shayne watch their father on television each week, but when he doesn't come by to see them in person they feel abandoned.

The suit seeks a court order requiring Lorenzo to see his children during each week and to take them every other weekend. In addition, Michele is demanding money damages to compensate she and the children for the emotional distress he's caused them by staying away.

Lorenzo's publicist told reporters that Michele's charges were baseless. Said he, "Lorenzo has loved and supported his children for their entire lifetime and sees them regularly and as much as possible, and has since the day of the divorce."

Well, which is it? Was Lorenzo ignoring his first two children while he was entwined with his beautiful young girlfriend making a third? Or, especially given the timing of Michele's lawsuit so soon after the new lovechild was born, is Michele out to publicly embarrass and shame him as a continuation of their own acrimonious divorce three years ago?

Whatever the case, Lorenzo is paying for his libidinous lifestyle now. It goes with the territory, though, in the ro-

mance-filled and exciting life of the dashing son of Hollywood's most famous Latin lover.

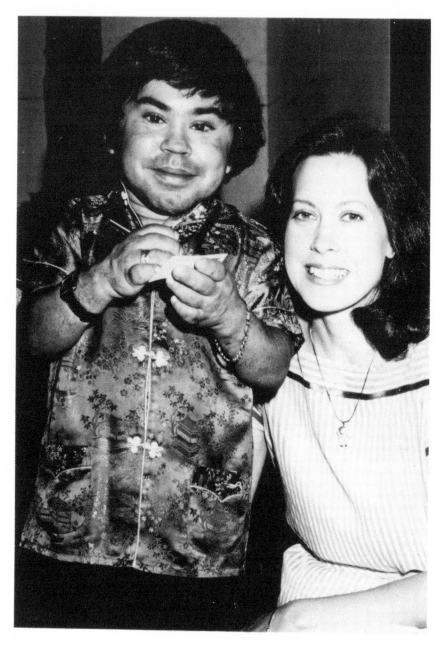

Herve Villechaize and his wife at a reception for ABC
affiliates in Los Angeles. (Scott Downie, Celebrity Photos)

Chapter 7

Herve Villechaize

The ABC-TV series *Fantasy Island* premiered in 1978 with Ricardo Montalban as Mr. Roarke and Herve Villechaize playing the part of the midget, Tattoo. Each week's plot had Roarke granting peoples' wishes and letting them live their innermost fantasies during weekend splurges on the isolated tropical island.

But while little Tattoo was helping dispense joy and fulfillment to hundreds of frustrated souls who sought refuge on the island, his soon-to-be ex-wife was taking action that would insure his own personal life was a living hell. He starred in *Fantasy Island*, all right, but he lived a *Nightmare on Elm Street*. When it was all over, he was ruined. Humiliated by her sensational accusations, his standing in Hollywood was destroyed. His fans turned on him, he lost his job, a national magazine parodied his sex drive and mocked his manhood, and his estranged even sued him for wife beating. He was quoted by a national tabloid as revealing he'd been violently arrested and hand-cuffed on the streets of Hollywood outside a popular restaurant, and thrown in jail like a dog for refusing to accept service of even more legal papers.

Herve is a native Frenchman who was born the son of a noted surgeon and raised on the Continent. None of his siblings is a dwarf; he is the only one in his family who didn't grow to normal size. He was trained as a painter at prestigious art schools and is in fact a skilled artist. Those few people who know him say he's extremely sensitive, quiet and private. There's no doubt he has been disadvantaged and ridiculed because of his size. After all, life in a world of six footers can't be easy for someone 3'9". But Herve never let his handicap keep him down. He went right out and competed in a tall world where one's physical appearance is absolutely key--show business.

A scene stealing role in the James Bond adventure *The Man with the Golden Gun* was Herve's first big break. He played Nick Nack, the devilish manservant of the villain

Scaramanga, and won enthusiastic critical acclaim for his performance.

From there, it was on to *Fantasy Island* to star opposite Ricardo Montalban in that offbeat new ABC series. As Tattoo, he scampered about the island in crisply starched dress whites and was the perfect foil for the omnipotent Roarke. While Roarke was the dream merchant whose supernatural powers propelled the weekly island odysseys, Tattoo also had his place. Foremost among his duties were aerial reconnaissance ("Da plane, boss, da plane") and playing straight man to Roarke ("What's the next visitor's fantasy, boss?"). The on-camera chemistry between them indeed clicked and there was also something about a midget at the controls of the island that gave the show an additional dimension of eeriness.

A 1977-78 mid-season replacement hesitantly wedged in the ABC line-up as a gamble, *F.I.* stunned everybody in Hollywood when it took off like a rocket in the ratings. An instant hit across the country, it made Herve a celebrity. Wherever he'd go, screaming fans would scramble to get a closer look and touch him. He was so tiny that one clamoring group of adult autograph seekers nearly trampelled him to death. Concerned for his safety, the network hired a bodyguard.

But, as it turned out, he didn't need protection from strangers . . . he needed it from his ex-wives and from a snobbish full-size Beverly Hills society which wouldn't accept a midget. To the millions of viewers around the country who would tune in *F.I.* on Saturday nights, Herve was a popular star. The entertainment industry's upper crust, however, gathering frequently at opulent private clubs and parties, derided him and laughed at the thought of him trying to have sex with a woman twice as tall as he.

In that environment, to this day, his personal, off-screen life has been tormented.

Item: Herve's eight-year marriage to 5'4" artist Anne Suzanne Villechaize ended in divorce in 1979. Herve blamed the abuse his wife got for being married to a midget.

Item: The February, 1980, issue of Hustler magazine featured a four-page cartoon parody titled "Ecstasy Island." In it, cartoon characters looking just like Montalban and Villechaize, with names changed to Mr. Dork and Taboo, rutted their way around the island, engaging in every conceivable sex act with a variety of partners.

Herve's character Taboo was singled out for especially harsh treatment. The midget in the cartoon first tells Mr. Dork that his fantasy is to finally get some sex and, of course, his wish is granted. The next frame shows two naked hookers ripping off Taboo's clothes and training a magnifying glass on his penis to try to locate it. Says one of the disappointed maidens, "I think we've been short-changed." The other, even more determined, produces a tape measure, chalks Taboo's manhood at two inches and shrieks, "God, he's hung like a hampster."

Rejected by the girls, Taboo turns his affections to the animal kingdom and has intercourse with a willing pig and then a monkey.

Absolutely outraged, Herve sued Hustler for $6 million, claiming he had wrongfully been depicted as a "compulsive sexual deviate." Pointing out that the cartoon portrayed him engaging in homosexuality, bestiality and sodomy and that it implied he was afflicted with priapism (continuous erection of the penis), he protested that its publication caused him to be shunned and scorned in Hollywood. Herve's lawyers calculated his damages as including $1 million for shame, mortification and embarrassment, $1 million for emotional distress, and an unspecified amount for damage to his acting career.

Item: Later in 1980, Hustler filed a formal answer to Herve's lawsuit and argued, in its defense, that the cartoon was truthful! And, said the lawyers for Hustler publisher Larry Flynt, "the statements . . . were made in obvious good humor and as a joke and thus did not carry any defamatory meaning."

Item: After spending four years trying to win his case and getting absolutely nowhere, Herve filed a statement with the court revealing he'd be willing to call off his $6 million suit if <u>Hustler</u> would pay him $30,000 for lost income and $1,000 for doctor bills.

Item: Four months later, worn out and unwilling to fight any more, Herve asked the Judge to throw out his lawsuit. The Judge complied.

Item: When <u>People</u> magazine sent a photographer and a reporter to interview Herve and his new bride, Donna Camille Villechaize, shortly after their September, 1980, marriage, they went straight for the height story. The gossipy weekly rushed into print with the news that the new Mrs. Herve was 5'8" and that Herve himself was now at 3'10". A full-page photograph showed Donna Camille as a very attractive 23-year old with long brown hair and trim physique. She and Herve were walking hand-in-hand. . . he came up to her waist. Home for the newlyweds was Herve's 1.5 acre San Fernando Valley ranch, where they kept chickens, ducks and horses.

Asking the questions everybody in Tinsel Town was laughing about, the interviewer got right to the point: Where and how did they sleep together? Well, replied Herve, the two of them jump into one twin-size bed for the night. The photographer sticks his head in the bedroom and snaps a shot of the tiny marital bed, which then appears as the second full-page photograph in the article.

In an unusually serious and probing exchange, Herve adamantly denied that he had storage disease, which afflicts many dwarfs and sometimes causes mental retardation. He refused to accept the interviewer calling him a dwarf, arguing instead that he was a midget.

Donna chimed in, "We're no different from any other married couple--except that usually the husband is taller than the wife."

Item: (The One Punch) On December 30, 1981, after fifteen months of marriage, Donna Camille filed for divorce. In it, she attempted to perform a walletectomy on Herve, demanding one-half of everything he owned, a chunk of what she estimated to be his monthly income of $100,000, their 1977 Cadillac, all the antiques and furniture, and $6,000 a month for her living expenses.

Item: (The Two Punch) As Herve was being sucked dry financially by Donna Camille's lawyers in the divorce settlement negotiations which left him, as he was quoted later as protesting, with only one dollar in the bank, she filed a second lawsuit against him. In it, she sought $325,000 for wife beating. The complaint she filed at the Los Angeles County Courthouse charged that when Herve would get mad, he'd take out his pistol and open fire on her. (Obviously, he wasn't much of a marksman, and she lived to tell the tale.) Too, her suit claimed he "on various occasions . . . struck, choked, imprisoned and otherwise assaulted" her. And on top of all that, she told people the other thing he'd do when he lost his temper was shove her in the fireplace.

She withdrew her lawsuit a few months later, so a judge and jury never got the chance to hear the evidence and decide if she was telling the truth. The jury might well have been suspicious upon learning that Donna Camille, at 5'10" and in great shape physically, was employed as a stand-in for tough *Charlie's Angles'* star Kate Jackson. Mrs. Villechaize, it turns out, was some kind of agile, strong stuntwoman who had certainly received an education from the Angels on martial arts, weaponry and hand-to-hand combat.

Visualizing 3'9" Herve, in a fit of rage, reaching up and punching her knees would be one thing, but overpowering her and heaving her into the fireplace is another. And, she claimed he'd "choked" her. Where? On her thighs? He would've needed a ladder to even see her throat and presumably an Angel could easily have knocked the ladder out from under him and in that way broken his leg. It all just seems preposterous.

Merely filing the lawsuit did real harm to the little actor, though, because all the newspapers reported the lurid allegations. Herve was branded as a wife beater and suddenly his fans turned on him. One woman came up to him in a restaurant one night, snapped, "You're the one who tried to kill your wife," and punched him right in the nose. His professional standing in the community was also damaged, as

Hollywood's power brokers began avoiding him. He even lost his job on *Fantasy Island* within a year in a bitter dispute.

It got so bad that Herve was forced to buy $5,000 worth of newspaper ads in Los Angeles denying the wife beating charges. He told reporters that the case was a pack of "sick and ridiculous" lies and he took his case straight to the people to try to clear his name. In the ads, he told readers that the lawsuit was so unfounded that Donna Camille had dropped it and that she had apologized to him for all the negative publicity it caused. But $5,000 in ads can't erase $1 million in sensational headlines and the dye was cast. His career was ruined. He'd been brought to his knees.

Today, Herve is a broken and defeated man. The light of his star has gone out--he's been out of work for years and blacklisted by the major studios and networks. He still lives on the ranch with his chickens, but the place is up for sale. What he wants to do is move to a small town and spend his days painting. For now, he volunteers his time as a counsellor for kids who are in trouble.

Looking back on it, Donna Camille must think Herve is a real loser. Most of the Hollywood elite probably agree. There are, after all, winners and losers in every fight. When he was on the top, Herve once made an offhand comment to TV Guide that he, underneath it all, was a fighter. He told them: "They think that if you are small you won't open your mouth. But I will fight for my rights."

In the years that followed, he fought for his rights in the divorce from Donna Camille, and lost; fought for the continuing affection and support of his fans in the face of wife beating charges, and lost; and fought a wealthy national magazine which belittled his size, and lost. But maybe if you're 3'9", just having the guts to stand up for your rights is winning.

The real story of Herve Villechaize is of a midget, doomed at birth, who picked himself up and competed one-on-one with the six footers and 42-longs of this society and made a success of himself. But even when he was on top, Hollywood was laughing at him behind his back. Their unending cacophony of sex and marriage jokes was cruel discrimination against a person who had no control over how tall he would grow.

Ironically, Herve was asked at the time *Fantasy Island* first aired what his own personal fantasy was. He replied in plain terms: "I want most to be treated like a human being." That's one wish the show never granted.

A grim Washington Redskins quarterback Joe Theismann
recounts his team's 38-9 loss at the hands of the Los
Angeles Raiders in the locker room at Tampa Stadium after
Super Bowl XVIII. (AP Laserphoto, Wide World Photos,
Inc.)

Chapter 8

Joe Theismann

For thirteen long years after his 1970 graduation from Notre Dame, Joe Theismann's destiny as football's golden boy was denied him. Yet his marriage remained rock solid all that time as young wife Shari dutifully nursed him at home in bed after games, covering his bruised body with hand packed ice bags.

On January 30, 1983 Joe snapped his football tailspin when he powered the Washington Redskins past the Miami Dolphins 27-17 in that year's electrifying Super Bowl. He finally made it.

His marriage didn't.

It's a classic case. Until Joe won the Super Bowl championship for the Redskins and was knighted the hottest pro football celebrity in the country, his marriage had held tight along the roller coaster of his career.

There were good times and bad times. They got off to a Cinderella start when Joe, the flashy quarterback of Notre Dame's Fighting Irish, married Shari during his senior year in college. He was the campus football hero who had it all-- muscular good looks, brains and charm. She was the former high school homecoming queen from Michigan who Joe described as the foxiest blonde on campus. Under Coach Ara Parseghian, Joe broke twenty-three football records at Notre Dame and was heralded nationally as the main contender for that year's Heisman trophy as college football's best back.

But Joe finished second to Jim Plunkett of Stanford in the Heisman balloting and his career took a nose dive because of it. He was passed over until the fourth round of the National Football League draft and ended up as quarterback of the Toronto Argonauts of the chilly Canadian Football League. He earned his stripes in Canada, though, setting passing records and restoring his self-confidence. After three seasons there, he returned to the United States and the Washington Redskins with his head high.

Some who were there in 1974 said it was too high. As soon as Joe hit town, hired on as the new lowly third-string QB to warm the bench while the team's veterans carried the mail every Sunday, the cocky kid opened a preppie restaurant ("Joe Theismann's") and eagerly solicited local newspaper and broadcast interviews. The joke among radio and TV sportscasters was that Joe never met a microphone he didn't like.

What he especially enjoyed talking about was himself and his successes at Notre Dame and Toronto; and his enormous ego was fed by the publicity he generated. Pushing himself into the limelight angered many of his new teammates, including senior starting quarterbacks Sonny Jurgensen and Billy Kilmer. Kilmer admitted that he and Sonny, once fiercely competitive as to which of them would start each Sunday's game, agreed that they didn't care anymore who started as long as it wasn't Joe. Referring to Theismann's mouthy arrogance, Kilmer asked Sports Illustrated interviewers: "Have you ever heard of a Notre Dame quarterback who didn't think he knew it all?"

Kilmer and Jurgensen, the leaders of the team, reportedly wouldn't even speak to Joe at their weekly meetings. He was totally ostracized. Joe even denigrated popular Coach George Allen at a booster club dinner one night; and his sharp, disrespectful comments were printed in the local newspaper the next morning. When Joe read that paper, he knew he'd be warming the bench a few more years.

Though few would speak to him civilly in the Skins' locker room during the day, Joe always had Shari waiting for him when he got home. A pillar of strength and support for him during the lean years in Washington, she carried him through. They had three beautiful children in this time, too--Joey, Amy and Patrick; and Shari made the home for the family and raised the kids.

Joe kept going back to the Redskins' training camp day after day, week after week and season after season to sit and brood on the bench. He waited for four seasons for one of the starting QB's to make a mistake, be injured or otherwise have to be replaced. He finally got his chance in

1978 and played so spectacularly that he never lost the lead position until he was injured in 1985.

By the end of the 1979 season, statistics showed no Redskins quarterback in ten years had thrown as many touchdowns and completions as Joe. The same team that wasn't even speaking to him the year before voted him that year's most valuable player.

Not only did Theismann have an arm like a cannon that could drill balls right on the numbers to quick darting receivers, he was an intelligent field general. He would methodically prepare for games by watching films of opposing teams with Shari. Then, the two of them would critique the other team's strengths and weaknesses. As they talked, Joe would diagram plays and plan strategy for the Redskins to use against what they'd seen on film. Shari would always go to his games, too, and cheer him on. She was a good football wife.

It was exciting to watch him play because he was such a master. His catlike agility and quickness eluded charging defenders and his laserbeam passing put games away for the Redskins. His throwing was so awesome that he became the number two ranked quarterback in the entire National Football League. The whole team caught fire behind his lead and they started winning big in a conference long dominated by the Dallas Cowboys.

They won the NFC championship in the 1982-1983 season and, with a barrage of Theismann-perfect passes, beat the Miami Dolphins in the 1983 Super Bowl to be crowned national champions. Joe was voted the most valuable player for the year in all of professional football.

Overnight, Theismann became a national celebrity as the hero of the Super Bowl. Good looking and bright, he was the perfect media icon speaking to press conferences, attending ceremonies at the White House and riding floats in televised parades. Having sought publicity his whole life, he reveled in the attention.

Confiding to Shari that he was in the sunshine now and there was hay to be made, he cashed in on his new celebrity status. He made several television commercials plugging products from cameras to tennis shoes, delivered motivational speeches to conventions for $4,000 each, was a popular guest on television and radio interview programs and actually was named to host his own local TV show-- *Good Morning, Washington.*

Joe was invited to some high-voltage Hollywood parties and was a big hit socializing with the stars. Brassy, talkative and cocky, he fit right in. He made several friends there, including Burt Reynolds, and they partied together like longtime buddies. Burt even offered Joe a role in his new film, *Cannonball Run II*, and the photogenic quarterback became a movie star in his own right. Joe was such a smash on the California star scene, and he was so obviously thriving in the limelight and public attention, the press began calling him "Hollywood Joe."

He lived up to the name, too. He wore solid gold cuff links in the shape of his jersey number, had four agents working for him and criss-crossed the country making personal appearances and giving speeches. He loved signing autographs and being recognized by strangers when he traveled.

Joe's jetsetting took its toll on his family life. He wasn't home as much anymore. And, when he did come back, could it be that plain old Shari just didn't compare to his new exciting Hollywood friends?

But by the autumn of 1983, he was again in the wing-T at Redskins Stadium throwing winners and marshaling his team to an impressive 14-2 record, a second consecutive NFC championship and Super Bowl berth. In that 1984 Super Bowl, however, the Los Angeles Raiders shut down the Theismann Air Force and thumped the Skins resoundingly for a stinging finale to the season. The rest of his year went straight down from there.

In March, he split from his wife and began dating Cathy Lee Crosby, the voluptuous Hollywood TV star of such T-and-A productions as *Battle of the Network Stars*, *Circus of the Stars* and some Bob Hope USO tours where she paraded to the delight of panting, whistling GI's.

The way Joe left Shari after 13 years of marriage angered many in Washington--he simply had the Redskins publicity office issue a press release announcing the separation. He hadn't bothered to mention it to her personally at the breakfast table, so she exploded when she heard it on the news.

She thought Joe was an ungrateful jerk for kicking her in the teeth like that and trading her in for a new model after all she'd done for him.

As Joe and Cathy Lee brazenly partied and played together all over town, and as the press dutifully chronicled their mating season as closely as it had Ling-Ling's and Sing-Sing's out at the National Zoo, Shari was on high simmer. She bit her tongue in silence, though, until Joe and Cathy Lee pulled a meat grab on her.

According to Shari, Joe did ads for a local meat company and, even after he left Shari, the outfit continued sending six boxes of meat out to his home each month. When Cathy Lee found out about the steakburger perk, she persuaded Joe to have the company send all six boxes to a drug rehabilitation center in California which she supported. When the next month's burgers for her three growing kids didn't arrive, Shari called the meat people and was told the dirt. She went into a white hot rage and, from that point on, she never missed an opportunity to stick it to Joe whenever reporters would ask her about the divorce.

She posed for the cover of the local glossy magazine Washingtonian tearing apart a photograph of Joe, complaining he was nothing but a gutless, shallow publicity seeker. She told reporters the reason for the divorce was that he couldn't handle his new found fame. Success changed him. She described him as "weird" to the Washington Post and told them she didn't know how she stood him as long as she did.

Cathy Lee didn't get much better reviews from Shari. To understand how Shari must have felt about the thought of her little children growing up with Cathy Lee as their stepmommie, more needs to be reported about the girl who first rode into the nation's consciousness bareback on a horse in a Velamints commercial. Tall, blonde and built, she is slinky and seductive. Cathy Lee reigns as one of Hollywood's hottest sexpots. Quipped Shari to reporters, "Would you want her to bounce your kids on her knee?"

Joe, by contrast, was uncharacteristically quiet through most of 1984, even to the point of quitting his radio and TV programs and cutting off his public appearances. He refused to grant interviews amid press speculation that he wanted to save his children the embarrassment of seeing he and Shari fight out their divorce in the newspapers. The mouthiest quarterback in the NFL abruptly went silent. Sports Illustrated heralded the phenomenon by running a picture of Joe on its cover with two pieces of tape superimposed over his mouth.

Regardless, the local press gave Joe a drubbing and public sentiment was running overwhelmingly against him. The people of Washington, D.C. love the Redskins and take personal, intense pride in the team. The team represents the city. For the Skins' quarterback to dump his loyal football wife for a Hollywood starlet just didn't sit right with the rank and file Redskins fans.

On July 14, Shari and Joe signed a permanent separation agreement which divided their assets. Shari got custody of the children, the $695,000 McLean home and a Ft. Lauderdale condo valued at $200,000.

Joe walked away with enough money to buy a picturesque 103-acre farm outside nearby Leesburg, Virginia.

A few months later, on March 28, 1985, their fourteen-year marriage was officially dissolved during a twenty minute no-fault divorce hearing presided over by Fairfax County Circuit Judge Quinlan Hancock.

Joe went back to playing football, but this time with the luscious Cathy Lee peering down on the play action from the owner's private box high atop RFK Stadium. Turns out, she was a jinx. The Skins went 11 and 5 in the '84-'85 season--their worst finish in years.

But if his passing wasn't quite on, their relationship sure was and by the start of the '85-'86 season the following year, Joe announced their engagement. He arrived for training that year a new man--calm, quiet and at peace with himself. Cathy Lee, he explained, was changing his life and slowing him down. She had made him abandon his frenetic pace and smell life's roses. Hollywood Joe had become a kicked back Marin County Joe, and the guy under that number 7 jersey just wasn't the same.

Three months later, in December 1985, tragedy struck in a nationally-televised game against the New York Giants. In the second quarter, Joe went out for a lateral pass from teammate John Riggins and was gang tackled by the Giants' beefy front line. At impact, his right leg shattered like a pencil. Millions watching the game on TV and in later replays of the gruesome episode actually saw the leg bend back below the knee and snap. Rushed off the field on a stretcher to a waiting ambulance, Joe refused painkilling drugs. His only request: "Don't let me go to the hospital without Cathy Lee."

ABC's Ted Koppel, who had been watching the game with her, frantically led her to the ambulance and it sped away. Once at the hospital, Theismann asked for a television set and actually laid there waiting for emergency surgery watching the Redskins win one for the lipper 23-21.

Cathy Lee stayed with Joe in his hospital room around-the-clock for eleven days. Press photographers snapped him in a huge leg cast, on his back in traction, with Cathy Lee shoehorned into the narrow hospital bed passionately embracing him. She told People magazine, "No matter what happens, even if it's adversity, we know we have each other."

Vowing that he was not going to let the injury end his football career, Joe began an intense rehabilitation program. After several months, however, it was clear that determination alone couldn't mend broken bones and he was put on waivers for the 1986 season. He didn't pass the annual NFL physical in November, 1987, and was declared medically ineligible to play professional football. No one anticipates he can recover from his disability to ever play again. From here on out, he'll be calling plays from the broadcast booth of ESPN on Sunday afternoons.

He says he's never been happier at home, though, and speaks of his relationship with Cathy Lee like a high school freshman would of his first date with the most gorgeous girl in the senior class. He confides that it is from the love of his children and Cathy Lee that he draws the strength to go on.

Shari remains bitter. Commenting on Joe's injury and hospitalization, she cracked to reporters, "I felt bad about him breaking his leg, but for the first time in 16 1/2 years, I know where he is and who he's with."

Pete Rose of the Cincinnati Reds. (Photo: the Cincinnati
Reds)

Chapter 9

Pete Rose

In 1963, Mickey Mantle and Whitey Ford nicknamed young Pete Rose "Charlie Hustle" during Rose's first season in the major leagues when he ran to first base on a base on balls during an exhibition game. Sixteen years later, Pete's wife Karolyn filed for divorce, claiming Pete hadn't limited his hustling just to the baseball diamond. Had he been chasing young women after ballgames for years in different National League cities?

Karolyn had been an avid fan during all of Pete's exciting years with the Cincinnati Reds. She went to most of his home games and would frequently be seen on national television cheering the Reds on with deafening two-fingers-in-the-mouth whistles and waving arms. She was there for hundreds of Pete's record-shattering hits.

The personal story of Pete and Karolyn's marriage is intertwined with the very public story of Pete's sensational baseball career. In fact, Pete has always acknowledged that baseball is his life. And Karolyn once remarked that if she had been a second baseman, she would've seen a lot more of her husband during their years together.

Pete will frequently tell Little Leaguers that it takes good eyes to be a professional baseball player. He was sure using his when he met Karolyn. As a young man, Pete was attracted to healthy chested women. At Cincinnati's River Downs race track one day in 1963 during his rookie year with the Reds, he was using binoculars to pan the crowd for sharp looking girls. Karolyn Englehardt was standing tall in a sheer blue miniskirt near the rail at the track. She stood out like a beacon of bosoms. Pete spotted her in his binoculars and was instantly attracted to her. He managed to learn her name (as it turned out, she worked at the race track as a bookkeeper) and arranged to be introduced to her. They began dating and were married a few months later.

After the 1963 season ended, Pete served six months on active duty with the Ohio National Guard. He and Karolyn planned their wedding for the week after he gradu- ated from basic training. The date they set was January 25, 1964. Pete went straight from the wedding ceremony at the church to a baseball writer's dinner where he was honored as the National League's Rookie of the Year. That meant for several hours, Karolyn was left alone at the wedding re- ception. Pete told the baseball writers that she accepted that as a baseball player's wife.

Being named Rookie of the Year fueled Pete's career. He'd earned that honor with a batting average of .273, hit- ting 9 triples, scoring 101 runs and stealing 13 bases during the year. Mantle and Ford obviously knew hustle when they saw it before the season began.

Pete still had several weeks Guard duty remaining after his wedding and Karolyn went with him. On the day his tour of active duty was up, the two of them drove back home to Cincinnati. But their time alone was cut short. That same day, Pete had to catch a flight to Tampa, Florida, to begin Spring training. It was Karolyn's 22nd birthday. Pete re- marked to Newsday's George Vecsey, "she was there with tears in her eyes; but that's baseball."

Even though baseball interfered with the newlyweds' first few months together, the game would give them enor- mous success in the years ahead.

Pete became a national hero the old-fashioned way--he earned it. It was a long road.

He signed with the Reds right out of high school, at age 18. The club then sent him to the minor leagues for two seasons. He never went to college; Pete was a self-made man. He grew up on the wrong side of the tracks in Cincin- nati and flunked his sophomore year of high school be- cause he horsed around too much and thought only about sports.

Later in his life, Pete would say that he and Ty Cobb had one important thing in common--how much they both loved their fathers. Pete's dad played semi-pro football for a Cincinnati team until he was 42. He was their kicker. One game, he broke his hip on the kickoff, but crawled down the field to try to make the tackle. It was that kind of hustle and determination that was drilled into Pete. Every Christmas, Pete was given a new baseball glove or basketball. Once, Pete's mother sent her husband downtown to buy a pair of shoes for Pete's sister. He came back with a pair of boxing gloves for Pete.

His dad instilled pride and the will to win in Pete which propelled him throughout his baseball triumphs.

During his early years in the majors, Pete attracted everyone's attention with his spirited, enthusiastic style. To watch Pete Rose play baseball was to watch a daredevil on the loose, a dynamo unleashed. Instead of running from one base to another, he slid into bases on his belly, head first in a cloud of dust. Rather than wait for a fly ball to come down so he could get a glove on it, he jumped like a trampoline-fired gymnast into the air to catch it. He was a daring base runner who lived to steal bases. He ran everywhere on the baseball diamond; he never walked. He gave the game everything he had. And nobody in baseball ever hit like Pete Rose.

The 1970s were good to him. Whether he was playing first base, second base or outfield, fans would fill stadiums to watch him hustle. He became a folk hero in his hometown of Cincinnati. Pete formed a partnership with fellow Reds standout Johnny Bench and invested his money right there in town. They bought a bowling alley, clothing store and an automobile dealership. He opened up two restaurants in town, named them after himself, and showed up there regularly to eat with his customers and sign autographs.

He drove a burgundy Rolls Royce around town with personalized "PETE" license plates. Locals would honk at him, and he would smile widely and wave back. He was the local boy who stayed in Cincinnati and made good. He never refused to sign an autograph for anyone who asked.

Pete led the Reds to a 1975 World Series championship over the Boston Red Sox in seven games and was named Most Valuable Player of the Series. Teammate Joe

Morgan told reporters that he'd never seen anyone who came to the ballpark with as much enthusiasm, desire and determination as Pete. Morgan said that to Rose, every day is opening day. He sure hit like it, his bat crackling out solid base hits with rapid fire consistency each season as he routinely broke batting records each year. He was voted the National League's Player of the Decade for the 1970's. He had the hot bat.

He developed a daily routine that worked. He'd sleep until noon or 1:00 p.m.; avoided watching too much television or many movies to save strain on his eyes; and didn't eat wimpy food like skimpy hamburgers, but stuck with good, thick steaks. He'd figure out his batting statistics each afternoon at the breakfast table and could recite them from memory. He'd get to the ballpark 6 1/2 hours before the game and go right to work getting in some batting practice. He was always the first player at the park.

Pete hated to take a day off because he lived to score a base hit. Reds general manager Bob Howsam once told author Bob Rubin that "Pete would run over his mother to get another time at bat."

Pete simply loved the game of baseball. He admitted that he played as aggressively as he did every minute he was on the field because he had so much fun. By the end of the 1970s, he was the highest paid baseball player in the country--earning more than $800,000 a year. He bought a beautiful mansion on 2 1/2 wooded acres in a fashionable Cincinnati suburb.

He wore his success well. He would tell people he was just thankful that he could make the kind of money he did without any college education. He was humble and was just glad to be where he was. Pete would often poke fun at himself and how he made all his money. "If you slid into bases head first for 20 years, you'd be ugly too," he would tell fans.

But everybody loved his face. The strong jaw, the gap in his front teeth and his Pageboy haircut were known to millions. His picture was on the box of Wheaties, the breakfast of champions. He could even be seen wearing only his colorful Jockey briefs and clutching a bat in a series of magazine ads for the well known underwear manufacturer. He became a national celebrity.

Those were also good years for Karolyn. Of course, there was no question she was a stunning woman when she married Pete years before. Five foot-two, slender and big chested, she was voted "Miss Popularity" of her high school class.

Before she met Pete, she wanted to be a go-go dancer or roller derby star. But as Mrs. Pete Rose, she capitalized on greater opportunities. She compared herself to Howard Cosell because she liked to tell it like it was and did a five-minute local radio sports show three times a day.

When Pete was named Reds captain, Karolyn took her role as the captain's wife seriously and would always make the first contact with a new player's wife to offer help and friendship. She was an unabashed, loud, cheering Reds fan. She gained national exposure during one playoff game in 1972 when she pulled off her sweater in front of live television cameras to reveal a skin-tight T-shirt which read "Big Red Machine" and which jiggled playfully.

Karolyn gave birth to a daughter, Fawn, in 1964 and a son, Petey, in 1969. She and the children would move to Florida with Pete each season for Spring training and, back home, frequently all show up to cheer him on at Cincinnati's Riverfront Stadium.

Pete was all baseball. When he'd come home at night after playing a late night double-header, he'd turn on the TV set and watch baseball all night long. But when Pete was on the road, Karolyn would worry about their marriage. When he didn't call home at night, her mind just raced with the persistent rumors of him being with other women. They apparently had fought about it and had reached an understanding--Pete was to be discreet when he was away.

She admitted being jealous of young groupies who would throw themselves on Pete when he travelled. "But what I don't know doesn't hurt me," she disclosed to <u>People</u> magazine, "just don't let me find out."

She found out enough in 1978 to leave him temporarily. The trial separation was triggered when Pete was named the defendant in a paternity suit. He didn't contest it and instead accepted the girl's allegation that he had fathered her child.

The marriage toppled with a bang the following year. The straw that broke the camel's back and drove Karolyn to finally file for divorce was that Pete was being seen in public right there in Cincinnati with a curvaceous blonde bartender. Pete had ventured over to Sleep Out Louie's Bar near the ballpark at the insistence of a clubhouse employee who whispered to him that the girl had the "prettiest butt in Cincinnati." Pete couldn't resist. And, after his own investigation, agreed with that assessment and began seeing young Carol Woilung, whose credentials included stints as a Playboy bunny and Philadelphia Eagles cheerleader before her barkeep job near Riverfront Stadium.

Karolyn couldn't believe Pete was doing this right under her nose in their hometown, and she stormed after Carol. She pounced on Carol one day in front of fans at the ballpark and ripped a diamond necklace off her. Karolyn slugged her in the mouth twice, splitting her lip.

Karolyn said that Pete's romancing of young Carol got so bad that she couldn't stand the embarrassment any longer and she filed for divorce in September, 1979. The official grounds, under Ohio law, which she cited in her petition were that Pete had "neglected his duty" as a husband. Translated to English, he'd been unfaithful.

Pete wasn't really his own best witness in defending Karolyn's charges. It was well-known among members of the press corps who had followed him for years that Pete always kept a keen eye out for good looking women. The truth was, he was notorious for it.

Trying to create an ordinary guy, anti-intellectual image for himself, he readily admits the only book he ever read cover-to-cover was *The Pete Rose Story*. Other than that, what he enjoys reading most are girl's T-shirts. He grinned when remembering for Esquire's interviewer a T-shirt he saw recently in Los Angeles. It read "Pete Rose, Number 14." "Man," said Pete, "she must have been a 38-C."

Does he really cheat on his wife when he's on the road? No way. "When you're a celebrity, they have you laying everybody," he explained to that same magazine. But can you ever really trust a baseball player who scratches himself in front of millions on national television?

Karolyn's mother, Pearl, a former vaudeville singer, thought it was a marriage made in heaven. Because no one else could stand to live with either of them, she remorsed.

But Karolyn left him and took the kids. There's no pain in life quite like it, either. Pete's response? Give it 110% at the ballpark. If you don't, he would say, you got no pride. He had his pride left, all right, and hit safely in 44 consecutive games, breaking a National League record. The only other person to have a longer streak was Joe Di Maggio in the American League with 56 games in 1941.

As he made baseball history that season, Pete acknowledged that no player had more personal problems or more injuries than he, but that he didn't want to take a day off to sulk. He was out on the diamond every single day giving it all he had.

After the 1978 season ended, the Reds didn't renew Pete's contract. Cincinnati was up in arms that the club Pete had played for his entire career would throw him out. Rose *was* the Reds and the fans were furious. Pete had it figured that the team's general manager at the time, Dick Wagner, was worried about image and let him go because of the paternity suit and his divorce. Pete lamented to Sports Illustrated, "You'd think I was the only guy in America to ever get a divorce."

The Philadelphia Phillies thought Pete's image was just fine, though, and signed him to a $3.5 million four-year contract in 1979 making him the highest paid baseball player in the country. Pete showed his mettle, too, leading the Phils to the 1980 World Series championship after a 97-year drought. In fact, he was winning the pennant and the

World Series at the same time Karolyn lowered the boom on him in divorce court back in Cincinnati.

By the time Pete and Karolyn got to the Hamilton County Court House for their July, 1980 hearing there wasn't much left to fight about. Karolyn took the witness stand and told Judge George Paul all he needed to hear. Pete was there with his attorney, but he didn't testify. Based on the testimony she gave, the Judge granted Karolyn a divorce, officially ending the 16-year marriage. She was given custody of Petey and Fawn.

Under Ohio law, parties are given several months after a divorce to divide up their property and agree to financial terms. Within five months, Pete and Karolyn entered into such a settlement agreement and it was then approved by the Judge as fair and equitable to all parties.

Karolyn got the $300,000 five-bedroom home in the suburbs, $72,000 in temporary alimony, $105,000 in cash, unspecified alimony payments which Pete would have to continue paying even if he died and the 1978 Rolls Royce. The local press put a $1.2 million price tag on her share.

In addition, Karolyn would receive $300 a month child support for each child. After they reached 18, the kids' full college tuition and all college expenses for four years would be paid by Pete alone. He would also be responsible for all medical and dental expenses of the children. In return, the Judge gave him the right to see his children at reasonable times as long as he gave Karolyn adequate advance notice that he wanted to see them.

Pete's share of their marital property included the 1979 Porsche, a house valued at $175,000, the $30,000 Hickock Belt for being named Outstanding Athlete of 1975 and all of his other athletic trophies.

Johnny Bench signed the property agreement as a witness for Pete.

Since the divorce, Karolyn has maintained relatively high visibility in Cincinnati refereeing professional wrestling matches and acting as a master of ceremonies at several sports clubs banquets. She says Pete refuses to talk to her since the split, but she is questioned even today by reporters about their highly-publicized divorce.

Karolyn admits that she still follows Pete in the box scores and that she's decided what makes him such a successful baseball player is the same thing that made him a failure as a husband--he has never grown up. She told ABC that when they were first married, she was Pete's third love. First, he loved baseball; second, his car. Then Karolyn. When Fawn was born, Karolyn was moved down to fourth place and when Petey came along Karolyn went to fifth. She resented being that low in the standings.

Karolyn is still quick with a jab when she gets the chance. In early 1989, when Pete was accused of illegally betting on baseball games and the I.R.S. and Baseball Commissioner's investigators closed in on him, Karolyn was one of the first to say anything publicly.

Reporters have asked Pete about Karolyn since the divorce, too, and his answers have been more civil. He gives her credit for being a good wife and a tremendous mother. He appreciates all the support she gave him at the ballpark through their 16 years together and how well she raised the children while he was on the road.

Pete is philosophical today and was quoted by the New York Times Biographical Service as saying that "the divorce wasn't her fault, but divorce is sort of a common thing these days, and it just happened that it happened to me."

In the years since his 1980 divorce, Pete Rose has become a baseball legend and one of the most popular sports figures of all time. He has a happy new family life, too.

He continued dating Carol. Then they lived together for a time. And they married in April, 1984. She was 30, he was 43. She gave birth to a little boy, whom they named Tyler after baseball great Ty Cobb. Why was Pete attracted to Carol, 13 years his junior? Because she made him feel young. She's been a new lease on life for him.

They bought a new chalet-style house on five acres of land outside Cincinnati. It has stables for Pete's four horses and plenty of garage space for his black 935 Porsche and shiny new red Corvette the team gave him in 1985.

In 1984, Pete rejoined the Reds as both a player and the team's manager. The hundreds of thousands of fans in Cincinnati knew that all was well again and they fired up for a rendezvous with baseball destiny. Because the talk of the town was that local hero Pete Rose was inching closer every game to breaking the legendary Ty Cobb's record, set in 1928, of 4,191 lifetime hits at bat.

He was a good manager, too, because he knew how to handle personal problems. What if one of his players' marriage was on the rocks? The local press quoted Pete as telling teammates in the locker room, no problem "just give her a million and tell her to hit the road." He would know.

But he was best at playing ball.

Billy DeMars, the Reds' hitting coach, was impressed by the Rose work ethic. DeMars revealed that Pete worked harder and practiced longer each day than anybody else on the team--and yet he was the oldest and one of the most successful hitters of all time.

There is something very special about the Pete Rose spirit and style. Sparky Anderson, the former Reds manager, believed that Pete was the best thing that had happened to the game of baseball since it was invented.

As he closed in on baseball's greatest record, Pete would unhesitatingly give credit to his dad for instilling in him hustling spirit. He often repeated that whatever he was and whatever he became, he owed it to his dad and to the game of baseball. He wants to be remembered as somebody who played hard, did his best every day and was a winner.

On September 11, 1985, Pete broke the immortal Ty Cobb's record when he cracked a first-inning line drive to left-center field in a game against the San Diego Padres at Cincinnati's Riverfront Stadium. It was the 4,192nd major league base hit for the 44-year-old Pete.

He bolted to first base. Once safe there, he thought about his dad watching him right then from heaven and he broke down in tears. His son Petey, the Reds' batboy, ran onto the field and they embraced, with tears streaming down. Pete told his son not to worry about it, that he'd break Pete's record some day himself. They held each other tight. The fans in the stadium erupted into a standing, stomping, screaming ovation that lasted seven full minutes. They had seen history with their own eyes, and their hometown hero had made it. The owner of the team brought a brand new red Corvette out onto the field for Pete.

His Reds teammates, all of the Padres and even the umpires swarmed around him.

He later topped off the night by scoring the Reds' two winning runs, adding a triple and ending the game with a sensational diving catch.

On the night of September 11, 1985, he told the hundreds of reporters who were there to record history that he'd never in his life cried on a baseball field before then. "I'm a tough son of a bitch, you know."

Five years after his ugly divorce, Pete Rose became the greatest baseball player in history. You can't keep tough sons of bitches down.

In 1989, Pete faced another serious personal crisis as allegations of illegal betting threatened to topple his career. As that dirty little scandal sizzles, Pete's hundreds of thousands of fans are standing behind him like they always have.

No one has done more for the game of baseball than Pete Rose, he's a man of the people and no mud thrown or charges brought at this stage are going to change any of that.

Bjorn Borg at the height of his professional tennis career.
(Photo: International Management Group)

Chapter 10

Bjorn Borg

Bjorn Borg spent his childhood learning to play tennis and his adolescence as a world-class champion. He started playing when he was eight years old and by the time he was 13 he had surpassed all young players in Sweden to win the junior championship and several other titles. When he was fifteen, he dropped out of school, saying that he hated the 9th grade and couldn't sit in a boring classroom all day when there was tennis to be played outside. He convinced his parents to let him forego a formal education to pursue his tennis career.

Young Bjorn received the finest instruction, training in Sweden and on the Riviera under the watchful eyes of veteran coaches. Lennart Bergelin, a brilliant player and coach, took Bjorn under his wing and guided his development into a tennis powerhouse before his 18th birthday.

This underdog schoolboy from humble beginnings took several spectacular tournaments, upending the top adult champions in Europe and was quickly touted by sports writers as the hottest new player on the tour. As his photographs began appearing in newspapers throughout Europe, he developed a huge following among teen-age girls who found him sexy. He was a made-to-order teen idol with boyish good looks, long blonde hair and shy manner.

But Bjorn led a quiet, reclusive life. Accompanied at all times by his coach, he spent his days playing in tournaments or practicing for hours at a time. After spending the day on the court, he would hole up in his hotel room. There, he would read Donald Duck comic books every night and listen to his collection of Elvis Presley and Beatles recordings. Explaining his rather boring personal life, he admitted to Sports Illustrated that "tennis is all I know, or want to know. It is my life."

He played Wimbledon two years after quitting junior high and was mobbed by a group of screaming schoolgirls who wrestled him to the ground on a London street. Wherever he traveled, girls would chase him. Yet, it was all for naught because they didn't understand that Bjorn was different from other boys in two important ways.

First, all that shrieking and pawing actually frightened this 17-year-old small town boy. In truth, he was extremely quiet and shy; and the onslaught of so many lustful girls just plain scared him.

Second, he made a conscious decision to forego girls for tennis. He would later write in his autobiography that "[e]very day I saw several of my friends . . . with . . . steady girlfriends, and each time I saw this, I thought to myself 'don't let this happen to me.'" He concluded "tennis and a steady girlfriend do not make a good combination." Ambitious and single-minded, he focused on tennis as a teen. At the time, he even said: "I myself am convinced that my career as a tennis player will come to an end the moment I feel as much for a girl as I do for that little white ball."

Strong words. The kind you often eat. Bjorn ate his two years later in the Paris springtime when a healthy-thighed Rumanian tennis player gave the champ an eye-opening lesson in love.

It was at the 1976 French Open, played at Roland Garros, that 20-year-old tennis machine Bjorn Borg began to notice new things on the courts. Women, namely. And love stirred within him after years of repressing it.

He was particularly attracted to Mariana Simionescu, a 19-year-old auburn-haired Rumanian with a slashing forehand. After several days of watching her on the courts and around the hotel, Bjorn telephoned her and introduced himself. It was the first time he'd ever called a girl for a date and he was at a real loss for words. Finally, he blurted out that he and his coach wanted to invite her to meet them in the hotel lounge later that night.

Bjorn's coach, Bergelin, helped the child prodigies feel more comfortable as the three of them talked in the bar. When the coach suggested the two youngsters make a night of it without him, Bjorn chose a strip joint as the best place to go. The atmosphere there, however, just wasn't right for quiet conversation on a first date and they quickly decided that a walk in the Paris evening would be more fun. They ambled around the parks and boulevards for hours talking about tennis and Sweden; and didn't return to the hotel until dawn.

Then, in a burst of instinct (because it certainly wasn't experience) Bjorn innocently asked Mariana up to his room for some cold Pepsi. She accepted and as daylight broke, he offered her a track suit to use as pajamas. There were two beds in his room and they jumped into separate ones as they continued their animated conversation. Mariana kept asking him questions but suddenly there was no reply--Bjorn had fallen dead asleep. She quickly leaped out of bed, dressed and ran to her own room. She opened the door to the horror of her mother, wide awake, who had been waiting up all night for her little baby to return from her first date with Bjorn.

Mom must have known lightning struck that night. Within two weeks, Mariana and Bjorn were inseparable. By that summer's Wimbledon championships, they were living together. Bjorn won his first Wimbledon title that year and credited his new serve, telling Time interviewers "I got Mariana and my new serve in the same ten days. I was pretty lucky." On November 4, 1976, they were engaged; and they officially married three and a half years later.

In 1976, Bjorn was 20 and on the threshold of brilliant years in his career in which he would earn the ranking as the world's top tennis player. To be sure, he was deeply in love with Mariana, but his devotion to tennis never waivered. Nor did their relationship dramatically alter his quiet life off the court.

For nine months each year, they made their home in hotels of tournament cities around the world. Bergelin would always accompany them.

Bjorn would awake each morning to breakfast and would rarely talk with Mariana. Instead, he would read two or three newspapers at a time and devour every word of the sports columns. Then, he and Bergelin would spend several hours practicing and training. On the days that Bjorn had matches, he would return to the hotel exhausted.

The three would always order their evening meal from room service and eat it quietly in the room. Then, a game or two of gin rummy before bed. Bjorn required ten hours sleep a night to replenish himself; but before her day was done, Mariana would wash out both her and Bjorn's tennis shorts in the bathtub and pack Bjorn's sports bag for the next day.

And on those next days, Bjorn wrote tennis history with his racquet. With a strong serve and burning ground strokes, he traversed the continents from one tournament to another playing with smooth precision. Along the way, he was very friendly and kind to others. Australian tennis great John Newcombe said Bjorn was "the nicest guy" he'd ever met and that he hoped his own son would grow up to be "as good a sportsman."

In sharp contrast to the childish flashes of temper of opponents McEnroe, Nastase and Connors, Borg was unemotional and impassive. In fact, his heart rate of 35 beats a minute was significantly slower than the average 72, and made him a serene machine. On the tour, it was said he had ice in his gut which made him cool and unflappable on the court. He was nick-named "Ice Borg" by some players.

Bjorn was polite and tranquil. He never whined or complained. He threw no tantrums and never bad mouthed an opponent. But as World Tennis reported in 1979, "Borg may not be a sonofabitch, but he plays like one." From 1976 to 1980, he became the first man in history to win five straight Wimbledon titles. He was the best in the world and simply dominated the sport in his twenties. He made more money each year than any other athlete in the world, bringing in an estimated $2 million in tennis winnings and another $3 million annually from endorsements of such products as tennis gear, cars, candy, cola, suntan lotion, talcum powder and airlines.

But in many ways, this shy, willowy young man had not changed drastically from the 15-year-old ninth grader who left school and home to seek his tennis destiny. Wherever he traveled around the world, he packed a brown stuffed toy bunny in his suitcase, calling it his "good luck bunny." And, he would always write letters home to his parents. Many of them sounded more like those from an unworldly young boy away at camp.

During their annual three-month hiatus from the tour, Bjorn and Mariana lived quietly in a three bedroom apartment in Monte Carlo. Fleeing Sweden to avoid exorbitant income taxes, Bjorn brought his parents along to Monaco and set them up in business there, operating the Bjorn Borg Sports Shop. Bjorn also purchased the small island of Kattilso, off the coast of Sweden, to use as a vacation retreat and rented a home on Long Island to give him a place to hang his headband when he traveled to America.

Yet, Bjorn lived conservatively and unpretentiously, lounging around the apartment watching TV.

The few times he did go out with friends, he was shy and quiet. Dr. Irving Glick, Bjorn's physician, was quoted by the New York Times Biographical Service as saying "he's not terribly educated, but he's very bright. He doesn't say a lot, but when he says something it's sound and basic."

Around the house, he kicked back in jeans and cowboy boots. In her book, *Love Match*, Mariana remembered her Viking best sleeping ten hours a day "naked, with no blanket at all." She revealed that "at first, I felt as if I was on an ice block." Her response was to wear two track suits to bed each night. Bjorn apparently did a lot of sleeping and Mariana a lot of watching. She later wrote "Oh, if you just could see him sleep. He's so quiet and relaxed. It reminds me of his little native town, Sodertalje."

After four years of living together and sleeping flesh to track suit, Bjorn and Mariana were married in an ancient Greek Orthodox ceremony in Bucharest in 1980. Mariana wanted to look like a princess, so Bjorn bought her a $7,000 dress. The ceremony itself was celebrated by four priests with a huge choir echoing their words. As was tradition, one priest placed a crown on Bjorn's head as the vows were exchanged. Mariana later wrote she whispered to herself then "my husband, the King."

He was de-throned in a year, and the amazing disintegration of their marriage was inexorably tied to an upheaval in Bjorn's professional life. At the end of 1981, he announced to a stunned world that he was going to take four months off the tennis tour to rest and recharge. His agent told reporters that after twelve years of intense training and competition, the Swede was "just tired of playing."

Bjorn himself excitedly told Tennis magazine interviewers that the layoff "will give me a chance of doing all sorts of things I have never had time to do before." He explained that the sport had required his total devotion and all of his time since he was a boy; and that he had not had a normal childhood. Strict coaches had deprived him of that. Now, at 25, in his own mid-life crisis he was going to make up for his lost adolescence. He was ready for some fun.

It was at that very point, though, after spending six long years together in cramped hotel rooms, that stress fractures surfaced in the marriage. Six years of four close walls and room service three times a day had been stifling. Six years of man, wife and coach traveling the globe, inseparable, and locked into a strict daily training and playing schedule that allowed little time for fun taxed their relationship to the limit. Mariana began to feel suffocated. So, in an incredible irony, at the peak of his career when Bjorn finally took time off to enjoy life, Mariana wanted a trial separation. She saw it as just some time apart to rekindle their love.

Bjorn would have to enjoy his layoff alone . . . and he did. Traveling to America to fulfill his product endorsement commitments, he became a born-again bachelor and, for the first time in his life, a party animal. European tabloids began reporting on his escapades. Once, he was spotted dancing at a New York City disco with a nubile model. Later, he partied all night with a comely belle in Charlotte, North Carolina. This was clearly wild oats time for Bjorn.

Mariana was unconcerned because, as she told World Tennis, "he's a house guy . . . he comes home. I just know that there is only one in his life and it's me."

When he did return home to Monte Carlo, he stunned Mariana, Coach Bergelin and his parents by announcing his complete retirement from competitive tennis. They couldn't believe it. This was not the same boy . . . this was a new Bjorn who had sampled life without tennis and enjoyed it.

He continued to travel extensively on business, endorsing products and making personal appearances around the world. Wherever he went, the tabloids and gossip columns back home made him out to be a snakemonster on the prowl for shapely vixens.

Mariana didn't stay in the apartment knitting a stocking cap for her Viking. Squeezing into a new wardrobe of skintight leather pants and short split skirts, she launched herself into the Monte Carlo nightlife. Sometimes escorted by other men and on other occasions alone, she stole the show at chic discos and wild parties all over the resort kingdom. She loved to disco and would frequently party all night, acquiring a reputation for being able to drink lesser mortals under some very fashionable tables in town. It was even reported that, in the daytime, Mariana would go nude sunbathing on the beach and race speedboats in the Mediterranean Sea.

Perhaps she was waiting at the docks for her explorer to return from the New World, but when the papers ran cozy photographs of Bjorn and 17-year old Swedish model Jannike Bjorling spending time together, she was quoted by Star Magazine as saying, "that was when I knew it was over."

Bjorn had met what one friend referred to as "the young one" at a Stockholm disco. He was there to judge a beauty contest and Jannike, tall and trim, was one of the contestants. She had long, shining chestnut hair and a body that wouldn't quit. Bjorn was absolutely infatuated. He was 27, she was 17 and his hormones exploded.

He had seen the future, and it was right there in Jannike's form-fitting Calvins. Recoiling at the thought of returning to his old life with Mariana, he told her it was over. They quickly hammered out the details of a friendly, uncontested divorce, giving Mariana what was estimated at up to $10 million of Bjorn's $40 million net worth.

Friends offered varying explanations for what had undone Bjorn and Mariana's love match. One of the most credible is that, despite repeated visits to fertility specialists on the Continent, Mariana was unable to have the baby that homebody Bjorn felt was essential for the kind of family life he remembered. In fact, having a child had been on Bjorn's mind for several years. Some saw his frustration with Mariana's inability to conceive causing him even more discontent when he quit tennis wishing to stay home and raise a family. There was no family to raise.

Others who saw it from the groom's perspective said Mariana was an untamed playgirl whose idea of having fun was going out dancing and drinking all night, chain smoking like a chimney from disco to disco on the arms of loud and obnoxious friends. By contrast, Bjorn was pictured as the quiet type who abhorred the nightlife, didn't like her plastic friends and preferred to stay home in front of the TV.

Mariana and her friends saw it differently. She protested that living with Bjorn hadn't exactly been a fairy tale. First off, she had to learn to speak Swedish and cook strange Swedish food to satisfy her Viking. Then, every day for six years she had to share her hotel room, her meals, her gin rummy games and her husband with Bergelin. It was an unusual triangle and Mariana was frequently the odd one out. Bjorn spent more time with his coach than his wife; and tension developed between the two as they competed for Bjorn's attention. Differences erupted as Mariana increasingly resented Bergelin's hold on her husband. She once even flashed her frustration to World Tennis reporters when she told them Bjorn "was so into tennis he forgot I was there." Those were the times, she confided to People, that Bjorn was "hell to live with." Divorce was the answer.

Bjorn squired the glamorous young one all over the world in 1984, including several weeks vacationing in Hawaii. In the fall, it was announced they were engaged. By winter, she was pregnant. In September, 1985, 18-year-old Jannike presented 29-year-old Bjorn with a beautiful baby boy, whom they named Robin Borg-Bjorling.

For the next two years, Bjorn was the family man he yearned so much to be. When he traveled on business, he took his family along; and Robin was easily spotted sucking his thumb in his stroller while dad played exhibition games or made appearances at cocktail parties talking with retailing executives about the many products he still endorsed. Wherever he went, Bjorn told reporters and fans that he'd never been happier.

But it didn't last. In 1987, Jannike left him.

And in early 1989, the sports world was jolted by news reports flashed from Italy that Bjorn had attempted suicide. Two versions of the incident were reported in later dispatches. One was that Bjorn had been belittled and rejected by his current girlfriend whom he'd planned to marry, Italian rock star Loredana Berte, and that he swallowed a fistful of sleeping pills to end his life.

The other version was that it was an accidental overdose. Either way, he was rushed to a Milan hospital where the doctors acted quickly to save his life. He was released later, smiling and wrapped in a huge blanket to keep him warm.

Today, Bjorn is living in Sweden and earning hundreds of thousands of dollars as the spokesman for ten major products worldwide. He's set for life in business; it's a peaceful family life which continues to elude him.

When just a schoolboy, he left home to achieve international fame and the admiration of millions. Since adulthood, he's been trying his hardest to make his own home life and recapture some of those lost years. He may be down two-love, but he's still young and can come right back with an ace. His fans want to see him do it, too.

Olympic decathlon champion Bruce Jenner. (Photo: Wallach Enterprises)

Chapter 11

Bruce Jenner

In 1976, Bruce Jenner won the coveted gold medal in the decathlon at the Montreal Summer Olympic Games and earned the title "greatest athlete in the world." He quickly capitalized on his fame, making a fortune endorsing products and starring in movies and television. But some say success toppled the private life of this innocent young man who got his start at tiny Graceland College, in the rural southern Iowa town of Lamoni.

By 1980, he divorced Chrystie, his college sweetheart and wife who had held down a job for four years so he could train for the Olympics. Tension mounted in their marriage when Bruce reportedly complained he never had any clean underwear anymore. One could see Chrystie firing back that he spent too much time out of his underwear anyway, and she protested that his accelerated sex drive was annoying her. She joined the National Organization of Women (NOW), started reading feminist literature and, after that, Bruce probably had to do his own laundry.

Within a month after leaving Chrystie, Bruce met and fell in love with Linda Thompson, the buxom blonde star of *Hee-Haw* who was best known as Elvis Presley's live-in girlfriend for five years before the King's death from a drug overdose. Bruce and Linda were soon married, had two gleaming children and separated five years later. Linda now says Bruce was always on the road leading the hectic life of a nationally-known celebrity. She simply didn't want to stay married to someone who was never home.

The not-so-dumb jock from Iowa who made history when he was twenty-six by winning the world's most prestigious Olympic gold medal, today at thirty-nine can count two marriages already which are also history. How could it happen?

Bruce attended Graceland on a football scholarship and majored in physical education. He met Chrystie during his freshman year and, being a bit shy and naive about women, took her to the laundromat on their first date. By their senior year, they were living together along with two other unmarried classmates. There they were, the two boys and their girlfriends, all cohabitating and cavorting in an apartment right across the street from the Dean's house. College can't get much better than that, but it was one secret they always kept from their parents.

As a college senior, Bruce competed in the decathlon at the 1972 Summer Olympic Games in Munich and came in tenth. He and Chrystie were married in December of 1972 and honeymooned in Iowa's capital, Des Moines, spending their wedding night at the Holiday Inn and eating dinner at McDonald's.

When he graduated from Graceland, Bruce set one goal for himself--to win the gold medal in the decathlon at the Olympics four years later. He would dedicate the next four years of his life to that quest and Chrystie was with him all the way. In fact, she got a job as a stewardess for United Airlines to support them.

They moved to San Jose, California, rented a modest $145.00-a-month apartment and made it their headquarters for the four year campaign that lie ahead. Bruce trained six to eight hours every single day. Typically, he'd get up early and run five miles to build his endurance. Then, he'd sell insurance until 1:00 p.m. to help supplement Chrystie's income. The rest of the day was devoted to working on techniques for each individual decathlon event. Hour after hour, Bruce would practice each sport. He'd always run sprints at the end and gut it out lifting weights, too. He would hit the showers by 7:00 p.m., but he didn't leave his work back in the locker room.

He was so totally preoccupied and consumed by winning the gold medal that it dominated his home life as well. He even set up a high hurdle in the tiny living room of their apartment to keep his mind on his task twenty-four hours a day.

But trouble began brewing in the marriage. According to Chrystie, it seems the more Bruce threw that javelin during the day, the hornier he was by the time he got home. At night, he'd constantly cling and follow her around. She finally demanded to know why his sex drive had increased and he responded that she was his wife now. And, that's what a wife was for. That he considered her his possession really grated on her.

Too, Chrystie complained that Bruce just didn't stimulate her intellectually. The guy heaved a sixteen pound shot for eight hours a day and she apparently expected him to come home and discourse with her on nuclear fusion. They would fight about money because there simply wasn't much of it; and that, too, put pressure on the marriage. And as Bruce's daily training intensified, Chrystie said he stopped helping her with work around the house. She held down a full-time job and yet he made her do all the housework and run the errands. She claimed he got so lazy that he wouldn't even take mail to the post office, and that she had to do everything. At one point in their first year of marriage, she actually walked out on him.

If there was ever a candidate for NOW membership, it was Chrystie and she joined up fast. Becoming deeply involved in NOW activities, she sought an identity for herself separate from Bruce. But was her new-found feminism straining the marriage, too?

Chrystie consulted a psychiatrist in California for some marriage counseling and it helped her cope. But beneath all of her frustration with the unending Olympic training, deep down she wanted that medal as fervently as Bruce did. It was her rainbow, too, and she was every bit as caught up in the chase for the gold as he was. In fact, whenever Bruce would get worn down and doubt that he could really pull it off, it was Chrystie who kept him going.

Superstitious, Bruce wore the same pair of "magic socks" in every decathlon he entered for six straight years. He thought they were lucky because he only lost one competition between 1973 and 1976 in those socks. A wife who would put up with the same stinking pair of athletic socks for six years is one who is committed to the marriage. Chrystie was. And she was committed to the dream, too.

Bruce struck gold on July 30, 1976 in Montreal when, in the last of the ten grueling decathlon events, he slashed through the tape at the finish line of the 1,500 meter run. Shattering three world's records during the day, he had taken the lead in the pole vault and finished strong by throwing the javelin and running the 15,000 meters better than he'd ever done in all four years of training. He was nothing less than bionic that day. As the other decathletes fell to the ground gasping for air after the last 1,500 meter run, Bruce leaped and danced his way through a victory lap to a tumultuous ovation from the thousands of spectators.

Suddenly, Chrystie broke through the police barricade and ran onto the field. She fell into Bruce's arms. "It's over," he told her.

When he got out of bed the next morning, Bruce quietly put the gold medal around his neck and stood in front of the hotel room mirror, naked, flexing his muscles.

But at that very moment, their best years together were already behind them and the few years they had left would turn bitter. Photogenic, talented and smart, Bruce parlayed his Olympic fame into a lucrative career as a TV sports commentator, movie actor and businessman. He peered out from the cover of Wheaties at millions eating breakfast, directed the Wheaties Sports Federation and delivered motivational speeches to conventions across the country for $7,500 a shot. In high demand for television commercials and magazine ads, he endorsed and advertised Minolta cameras, Norelco razors, Buster Brown shoes and his own line of sportswear.

He and Chrystie decided to reward themselves with a new luxury home and they found one for $200,000 in Malibu that had a swimming pool, tennis court, gymnasium and billiard room. When the local banker asked Bruce what he planned to put down to purchase such an expensive property after living in a $145.00 a month apartment for years, Bruce didn't flinch. "One gold medal," was his curt reply. He got the house.

His hustling paid off and the money started rolling in. He earned half a million dollars the first year after Montreal and bought such utensils of the good life as a white Porsche and a 6-passenger Beechcraft Bonanza airplane.

Cashing in on his status as the nation's newest exciting sports celebrity, Bruce was on the road twenty days a month. In great demand, he was constantly on the run fulfilling television and product advertising commitments. But was his success destroying his marriage?

While Bruce personally enjoyed the lifestyle and recognition of a public figure, Chrystie loathed living in a fishbowl with his millions of admirers looking on. He was home so few days a week with her, and was even then always in such a hurry, that Chrystie was quoted as grumbling he never had any time for her anymore.

Hating her new life, she decided to write a book about it so that everybody would know how miserable she was. In it, she grumbled that she had to spend all of her time running errands for Bruce, entertaining his friends and cleaning up after him at home. She wrote about how hard she had slaved for four years to get him through the Olympics only to find herself still working like a dog taking care of everything he needed in his new career. Bruce always came first and she never had time left over to do things for herself.

Chrystie told gossip columnists that she'd give her eye teeth to be back where they were before Bruce became a celebrity. But the marriage klinked along and Chrystie gave birth to a baby boy, Burt, in 1978. The baby added even more strain around the house, though, and the couple agreed to a trial separation in 1979. A few months later, they decided it was no use to try anymore; they would get a divorce.

But shortly after they announced their intention to formally end their marriage, Chrystie found out she was pregnant again.

Even in the face of the jolting news from Chrystie's obstetrician, the divorce was on. They talked it over and decided it would be wrong to stay together just for the sake of the kids. But when pressed on the point by Playboy interviewers, Bruce admitted leaving baby Burt made him sad "but it makes you feel even more guilty to leave a pregnant wife." Six months later, Chrystie gave birth to a baby girl, and they named her Cassandra.

When the lawyers entered the picture, things started to get nasty. Chrystie first asked the Judge to order Bruce to pay $60,000 in cash to her lawyers to pay them for the time they spent going after his assets. For her share of the marital pie, she asked for half of everything Bruce earned "as a world renowned celebrity [because his] fame was created during" their marriage with Chrystie supporting him while he trained for the gold medal.

In subsequent pre-trial pleadings and affidavits of sworn testimony, she demanded $10,000 a month in alimony and $5,000 a month in child support. To justify those amounts, she listed her monthly expenses for the Judge: mortgage payment on the house--$6,300.00; food for herself and two toddlers--$950.00; child care for the children--$868.00; costs of maintaining her cars--$615.00; clothing--$400.00; and utilities and telephone--$950.00. All totaled, it cost her more than $15,000 every month just to pay the household bills.

She said Bruce could afford to support her, too, because of his monthly take-home pay of $21,000, his $350,000 Wheaties contract, $250,000 Minolta endorsement deal and the $30,000.00 they had in their joint checking account. While the lawyers fought it out, Chrystie asked the Judge to prohibit Bruce from coming into their house and to restrain him from disturbing or molesting her.

Within a few months, they settled it all out of court. On November 26, 1980, Superior Court Judge Pro Tem John R. Alexander approved the division of marital assets agreed to by the parties which gave Chrystie the Malibu house which was by that time worth $1,400,000. She also got all the furniture and art in the house except the pool table and weightroom equipment which Bruce demanded. The new Toyota Celica and a cache of furs and jewelry were listed in Chrystie's column, as well as $15,000 a month in alimony for one year and then $5,000 a month in alimony for four years. Too, she was awarded physical custody of the two children and $2,000 a month in child support from Bruce to pay for the costs of raising them.

For his part, Bruce was given the right to visit his children at reasonable times and to participate in all decisions that could affect their education, health, religious training and development. He was expressly allowed to attend and be a part of his childrens' activities as they were growing up. He got the vacation home in Lake Tahoe, airplane, Mastercraft boat, go-carts, jet ski boat, 1979 Jeep, 1978 Ford van and two 1978 motorcycles. The biggest asset Bruce won was all the earnings, goodwill, residuals and contract rights "from his services as a professional athlete, TV commentator, actor and performer." He was also given his Screen Actor's Guild pension and the Lloyd's of London disability insurance policy he carried on himself.

Bruce revealed to Playboy how he felt about the settlement: "Don't let the press feel too bad for her; Chrystie will come away from this thing financially set for the rest of her life." He rented a place in Malibu within walking distance of the old house so he could be close to the kids and share the responsibility for raising them.

How could gold turn to guano so quickly between 1976 and 1979? Chrystie thinks that she had been forced to sacrifice too much for Bruce during their marriage. "I had to subjugate everything" for Bruce's career, she told reporters. She remembered running all of his errands for him every day and Bruce laying on the sofa watching TV; and the more she thought about it, the madder she got. Chrystie complained to Women's Sports magazine that for the four years Bruce was in training "I was supposed to supply absolutely everything emotionally, physically and financially." That just didn't sit right with her. She came right out with it in her book: "My heart goes out to all the women who have committed themselves to support their men for . . . years." On top of all the residual resentment of Bruce, Chrystie also had found it uncomfortable living as the wealthy wife of a national celebrity. The pressures of new wealth and living in the public eye simply made her unhappy.

Bruce saw it differently. "I don't like to think that success spoiled it," he told the Los Angeles Times, "people change." He figured that he wasn't even close, then in 1980, to being the same person he was when they were married and living in little Lamoni, Iowa, in 1972. He had matured into an adult who was, frankly, a different person than the unworldly college boy Chrystie had married. The years had changed him and he had grown at a different rate than Chrystie to the point that they were now incompatible.

Regardless of what caused the break-up, Bruce was fired by Wheaties as their spokesman after news of his divorce was splattered by the press on front pages across the country. Seems the corporate wheels at General Mills didn't think the public was ready in 1980 to sit down to breakfast with a divorced Mr. All-American boy smiling at them from those cereal boxes.

Shortly after separating from Chrystie, Bruce met Linda Thompson at a tennis tournament on Hugh Hefner's estate in southern California. Linda, one of the curvaceous farmer's daughters on TV's *Hee Haw*, was looking good. For five years up until 1976, the former Miss Tennessee Universe had been Elvis Presley's live-in girlfriend; and you've got to figure Elvis had taste in beautiful women. So, she had credentials. At Hef's place, Bruce spotted those credentials when he saw her from the back as she walked past him. "Wow, look at that!" he's quoted as exclaiming at the time.

He asked for her telephone number and they hit it off from the start. In fact, two months after Bruce's divorce from Chrystie was finally signed by the Judge, he married Linda in a beautiful sunset ceremony on Hawaii's Diamond Head Beach. His two year old son, Burt, was best man to the delight of those few family members and close friends invited to attend.

Home for Linda and Bruce was a spectacular multi-level log cabin they built on a rustic acre in Malibu. The home was designed in tune with nature; in the yard, there were waterfalls and wild flowers. The place also had a jacuzzi and separate swimming pools for the children and the adults. There was, of course, a fully equipped indoor gym for Bruce. They got along famously, cooing about each other whenever asked by the press. Bruce would say Linda was the nicest, warmest and most down-home girl he'd ever known. Linda often told people Bruce was consummately decent and kind. The storybook marriage in the California wild flowers produced two children--Brandon in 1981 and Brody in 1983.

When Bruce was asked while travelling in 1985 by the Chicago Sun Times the secret to his happy marriage, he didn't hesitate in responding, "bring[ing] home a good pay-check." Although he was surely bringing in big money in his travels, he was also having to spend time away from Linda and the children.

It grew so bad that Linda couldn't take it anymore and demanded a separation in 1986, sniping that the kids wouldn't even realize the two were living apart because their dad was always gone anyway. She confided that when he was home, Bruce was a very loving father; but he was simply so busy that he didn't get home often. She objected that she spent so much time alone with the kids that she felt like a single mother all those years.

On January 16, 1987, Linda officially filed for divorce in Los Angeles. But the couple remained on friendly terms and quietly settled the case out of court. Linda and her attorney appeared before Judge Kenneth A. Black on February 2, 1988 and presented him with a 46-page settlement agreement which had been signed by both spouses. Bruce didn't go to the courthouse and didn't even retain a lawyer. He had acted as his own attorney and did the negotiating with Linda himself.

If there was ever a civil, decent and truly uncontested divorce, this was it and Judge Black granted the dissolution effective February 22, 1988. The judge then issued a formal, 25-page divorce decree which incorporated the terms to which the parties had agreed.

In that decree, the joint or community property of the parties was split between them. Linda got the Malibu home and residences in Bartlett, Tennessee, and Monette, Arkansas. She was also given Bruce's E.F. Hutton I.R.A. and two of their snow mobiles.

Bruce got the Lake Tahoe home, the 1982 Beechcraft, all the stock in his 8618 Corporation and the other two snow mobiles.

Separate property set off to Linda included the 1982 Porsche, 1985 Ford station wagon and all her jewelry and furs. Bruce kept the 1977 Porsche and a 1980 Toyota land cruiser.

The division of assets and money wasn't 50-50. Linda got a bigger share because Bruce didn't want to have to write out monthly child support and alimony checks. So, Bruce agreed to pay the $83,000 owed on their 1986 taxes and to transfer large sums to Linda from his 8618 Corporation's retirement and profit sharing plans. Four trust funds at E.F. Hutton were also maintained for the children's benefit.

That satisfied Judge Blake, who wrote: "The Court finds . . . that the needs of the minor children will be adequately met by the provisions of this Judgment [even though Bruce will not be paying monthly child support directly to Linda]." Later, Black acknowledged that the unequal division of assets was "fair" given Bruce's wish to be relieved of alimony and child support payments and "that the parties intend each to separately meet the needs of the minor children for child support into the foreseeable future."

Linda and Bruce agreed that they would share joint legal custody of their sons, that Linda would be awarded primary physical care custody of them and that Bruce would share time with the children "at times as mutually agreed upon by the parties."

As divorces go, both Bruce and Linda deserve gold medals for ending their marriage so rationally and civilly. Millions could benefit from their model.

A dashing figure still very much a household name, Bruce today doesn't want for female companionship. He's been photographed in Hollywood and Florida with several curvaceous starlets, including--fresh from her sailboat ride with Gary Hart--Donna Rice.

Yet, privately, Bruce Jenner is a loving and caring dad. He's a modern father--nurturing, sensitive and involved hands-on in raising his children. He is decent and kind.

Bruce has been criticized, often in the heat of divorce or separation, for being on the road frequently, but it should be remembered that travelling is a necessary part of his job. He doesn't work 9 to 5 at a local store--he built a career with hustle and brains as a well-known and well-liked celebrity that requires him to get out in the public and travel.

While life in that fast lane has taken a cruel toll on his family life already, Bruce can always be sustained by his athletic triumphs. With guts and grizzle, in four grueling years he went from Lamoni, Iowa, kid-with-a-dream to greatest athlete in the world. As he said just before the 1976 Olympics, "I know if I win, they can never take that away from me."

Erik Estrada of "Chips," his wife Peggy and their son at the
Los Angeles premiere of the new Michael Jackson movie,
"Captain EO." (Scott Downie, Celebrity Photo)

Chapter 12

Erik Estrada

The week before teen heartthrob Erik Estrada was secretly married in 1979, he was pictured bare-chested on the cover of <u>People</u> magazine as the first of the ten sexiest bachelors in the world. The star of NBC's popular *CHIPS*, Estrada was invariably billed by the Hollywood press as sensual and lustful. Knowing a good body when it saw one, NBC packaged that raw physical appeal in a noticeably tight California trooper uniform and sent Estrada to stardom.

He was a made-to-order television sex symbol--smiling, coiffured and bulging. Quite the physical specimen at 5' 10" and 160 pounds, he lifted weights zealously, did 120 push-ups every day and ate fistfuls of vitamins at a time. It paid off . . . he was a hunk.

His teen-age fans couldn't be kept away. At the MGM studios, young girls frequently tried to break down his trailer door. When the show went out filming on stretches of southern California highway, fans would swarm around him and create chaos on the set as soon as they spotted the *CHIPS* trucks and cameras. Estrada drew more than 3,000 fan letters a week while his co-star, Larry Wilcox, got ten. He was hot.

His beginnings were humble and tough. Born and raised in New York's Spanish Harlem, his parents were divorced when he was two and his father moved back to Puerto Rico. Erik was raised by his mother, who was a seamstress, and they knew hard poverty during his childhood. Their neighborhood teemed with street gangs, knifings, druggies and hustlers.

As a boy, Erik shined shoes in New York's Coliseum to earn money. Later, he worked as a waiter. When he was in high school he was drawn to acting in an unusual way. He began going to drama club after school to follow a girl he was chasing and whom he wanted to impress with his own interest in theatre arts. But he enjoyed what he saw so much that he started acting and developed real enthusiasm for it. He forgot about the girl and pursued acting instead.

After high school, he enrolled in a special program for Latin-American ghetto children sponsored by New York City Mayor John V. Lindsey. One of 40 in the program, Erik was paid $32 a week to sing in Spanish and dance in the ghetto parks on weekends. During the week, he and the others were taught by accomplished performers and teachers.

Erik enrolled in the prestigious American Musical and Dramatic Academy after 1 1/2 years in the Lindsey program. He studied every aspect of show business during two years at American and, upon graduation, landed parts in such films as *Airport '75*, *The New Centurions* and *Midway*.

Estrada became a star overnight in 1977 at the age of 28 when he first appeared as motorcycle officer Frank "Ponch" Poncherello on NBC's *CHIPS* series. CHIPS, an acronym for California Highway Patrol, was one of the new non-violent cop shows. Larry Wilcox played Officer Jon Baker and each week's episode featured four or five separate plots ranging from the hot pursuit of a fleeing gunman to Ponch's social life.

Off the set, Estrada was flying high. Of his impoverished and sometimes painful childhood, he once said that it seemed he went from ages 5 to 23 with nothing in between. Now, with the instant wealth and celebrity status of a hit TV show, he was making up for lost time.

He reveled in the adulation of his teen-age fans and savored the attention of the press. He drove a Mercedes and a Rolls-Royce and lived in style. A dashing man about town as he squired nubile young women, he was known for showering his dates with costly gifts. Most were given elegant jewelry, but for one girlfriend with a dental annoyance he had one of her teeth capped in expensive porcelain.

Estrada's amorous appetite seemed insatiable. He would meet young women on the set or at the supermarket and ask them out. As one of Hollywood's hottest studs, few turned him down. He even proudly told <u>People</u> reporters that he enjoyed being picked up by women "if the picker is good." (His criteria for "good" were plentiful bosoms and tight buttocks, it was later revealed).

In the *CHIPS* program, Ponch was cast as the happy-go-lucky, good humored young bachelor who often exasperated his superior, Sgt. Getraer. But Estrada was no happy man when, while filming one episode in August 1979 he lost control of his 900-pound Kawasaki and was thrown face-first onto the hood of a camera car. The bike landed on top of him. In excruciating pain, he was rushed by helicopter to the intensive care unit at UCLA Hospital. There, doctors found the huge cycle had broken Erik's collarbone, breastbone, wrist and of his several ribs. On the critical list for two days, he looked like a mummy in his casts.

Twice, doctors told co-star Wilcox that Erik wouldn't make it. But Estrada fought for his life and recovered. A bull of a man after all those years of weight-lifting and as determined as anyone from his background would be to fight adversity, he would not be denied.

His fans were hysterical. Sixty thousand people sent letters and get well cards. There was so much mail that MGM had to hire an extra mailroom clerk. Five hundred well-wishers sent flowers; and telephone calls from as far away as Australia inquiring about his condition were received by the hospital at the rate of one every minute. To get closer, one fan even dressed up as a priest before being discovered as an impostor in Estrada's hospital room.

It had truly been a brush with death and Erik was lucky to be alive. But his life would never be quite the same.

Making a miraculous recovery, Estrada was out of the hospital in ten days and recuperating in the Hollywood Hills under the watchful eye of his 19-year-old girlfriend, who also happened to be a nurse. They were even pictured in his hospital bed together, reading get-well cards. Obviously, no 900-pound motorcycle was going to deprive this sex symbol of the company of attractive young women.

In a few weeks, though, patient and nurse split and Erik flew to Hawaii to continue his recovery. It was there in September of 1979 that he met and fell passionately in love with Joyce Miller.

After a whirlwind courtship, the two secretly married in Las Vegas on November 25, 1979. He was 30 years old and she was nine years older. Within a few days, news of the marriage of the most eligible bachelor leaked out. <u>Teen</u> magazine reported the shocking story to Estrada's millions of young fans with the analysis that his near-fatal cycle accident probably convinced him to slow up and settle down.

Seven months later, however, Joyce was out of the house, claiming Erik threw her out without money or clothes. Erik filed for divorce the next day in Los Angeles County Superior Court. And the turbulent story of those seven months slowly began to emerge in the documents each party filed with the court.

In his July 1, 1980, petition for dissolution of marriage, Erik cited irreconcilable differences as the reason he wanted out.

Two days later, Joyce asked the court to award her $5,000 a month in alimony and half of the $500,000 she claimed Erik earned during their seven-month marriage. She also demanded her community property half of all the assets of the parties, including their Studio City home, furniture, cash, life insurance, stocks, bonds and Erik's retirement pension.

Within a week, Joyce persuaded Judge D. E. Schempp that Erik was molesting her, disposing of her property and refusing to allow her to return to the home to pick up her personal belongings. On July 7, the Judge signed an order restraining Erik from molesting or disturbing Joyce and requiring him to allow Joyce to return to the home on July 9 for three hours to remove her personal belongings. The Judge even ordered Erik to remain at least 500 yards away from the house when Joyce was there.

Erik was outraged. On July 10, he signed a statement for Judge Schempp swearing that Joyce was the one who was out of control and needed restraining--not him. Erik explained that Joyce was telephoning him every day and insulting him. He said she would chew him out on the phone and then hang up.

Erik protested to the Judge that Joyce had gone on a spending spree in Los Angeles in the two weeks since they separated and that she had charged $2,300 worth of new clothing and billed $260 for perfumes in Erik's name on his charge accounts.

He charged that Joyce had run off with a 1978 Mercedes Benz 450 SL that really was leased by a film company. Erik reported that not only had Joyce refused to return the company car or tell Erik where it was, she had already been in an accident and damaged it.

Further, Erik explained that Joyce already was telling people terrible lies about him, including one story that on a night when they were fighting he threatened to kill her. She was complaining he pulled out a gun and fired a warning shot into the ceiling of their bedroom. He said the truth was that he was merely cleaning that pistol when it accidentally discharged and that Joyce was in another part of the house on the phone to a girlfriend at the time. That friend would later verify Erik's version. But what really concerned Erik, as he stated to the Judge, was:

> "Joyce is threatening to make her
> bizarre lies available to the press. I am
> completely at a loss to explain her
> motives; why she would want to hurt me
> is beyond my understanding. At no
> time have I attacked her in the press.
> I was good to her. I let her live her
> fantasies of wealth and fame. I
> simply could not live with her bizarre
> lies any longer. She should not be
> allowed to turn this . . . into a
> launching pad for a mindless, vindictive
> personal attack on me."

The Judge was convinced that Joyce might well smear Erik in the press over the divorce and on July 11, 1980, ordered both of them to refrain from making any derogatory or slanderous remarks about the other. He also made Joyce return the Mercedes in exchange for Erik leasing a Buick or Monte Carlo for her use. And, he ordered Joyce to stay away from Erik and to stop annoying and harassing him. To keep a lid on all of the potentially scandalous proceedings which the press might thirst for, Judge Schempp closed the court file to the public.

But on July 29, 1980, the National Enquirer stunned the nation with an expose of the Estrada divorce, as told to Enquirer reporters by both Erik and Joyce.

The article quoted Joyce as describing her marriage to Erik as a "nightmare" and seven months of "hell." She said she had lived in terror and recounted the episode with the pistol in their bedroom when Erik threatened to kill her. She reported he actually had thrust the barrel into her mouth.

Joyce told the magazine that Erik was so vain he'd spend hours staring at himself in the mirror, that he hated kids, had no friends, had never read a newspaper and that she had to read papers to him just so he'd know what was going on in the world. She revealed that he was so uncultured she had to teach him which fork to use, how to open a car door for a lady and how to walk properly.

Erik had married her for her father's money, she explained, and he had demanded expensive gifts from her during the marriage. She described him as terribly insecure and so dependent on her that she felt like his mother.

But the worst part of it, believe it or not, was Erik's physical appearance which Joyce found absolutely disgusting upon closer examination after they were married. She reportedly told the Enquirer that Erik had gross, scaly feet like a leper and that he would sit on the kitchen counter and pick at them while she was fixing dinner. On top of that, she complained that his back was nothing more than a field of ugly pimples which she had to rub with acne cream every night before bed.

For his part, Erik was quoted by the magazine as saying the marriage failed because of Joyce's lies. For instance, she had told him that she was European nobility (the granddaughter of Baron Guy de Rothchild) and that she had only been married once before. In truth, he said, she had been twice married and was certainly not related to any of Europe's blue bloods.

On December 12, 1980, while the attorneys for both parties were negotiating final divorce settlement terms,

Joyce filed a separate $1.7 million lawsuit against Erik for assault and battery and the emotional distress the marriage caused her.

Joyce's allegations were shocking and sensational. She claimed that during their brief marriage Erik had forced her to consume such illegal drugs as LSD, cocaine, heroin and marijuana; tied her with a rope and sexually assaulted her; tried to run over her with a car; beat her in a limousine; threatened to shoot her three different times and made her watch porno films.

She complained in her suit that Erik married her only as a publicity gimmick. Further, that he committed revolting sex acts and forced her to participate in cult Black Magic rituals with him where he painted her entire body with a fluorescent paint to glow in the dark.

The irony of it all, of course, was that each morning after, Erik would put on his California highway patrol uniform and spend ten hours making drug busts, quelling domestic disputes and saving damsels in distress.

Immediately, Erik's attorney labeled the charges "nonsense." Erik confided two years later that he wanted to telephone reporters and tell them that Joyce was lying but that he decided he wouldn't comment for fear of making it worse. So, he said, he just cried alone about what she was doing to him.

But a week later, Joyce dismissed her $1.7 million suit as part of the final settlement of the divorce action. A six-page interlocutory divorce decree was signed by Judge Richard E. Denner on December 16, 1980, and contained several terms. Erik and Joyce agreed that he would pay her $3,490 a month in alimony for three years, pay her attorneys $17,500 in fees for their representation and pay $16,800 of her bills. Erik, in turn, would get the Studio City home, the Tarzana home, full interest in his pension and the residual rights to his past motion picture and television performances.

The decree also specifically enjoined and prohibited both Erik and Joyce from harassing one another or making derogatory comments about the other to anyone.

After the Judge had signed the decree, Erik smiled and waived at several fans who were waiting outside the courtroom. Minutes after being divorced, both Joyce and Erik sounded conciliatory. He said he hoped he hadn't caused Joyce any problems. She apologized for filing the blockbuster assault suit, explaining she had been hospitalized and taking medication the day she signed it.

Yet the truce was short-lived. Within just a few weeks, Joyce went back to the Enquirer and protested that while they were married Erik had become totally egotistical and disgusting. She was glad their marriage was over and never wanted to see Erik again. When the magazine published the interview with Joyce on January 13, 1981, Erik screamed foul. He immediately filed a petition with the Judge asking that Joyce be punished for contempt of court for violating the Judge's December order that neither party defame the other. To support his case, Erik gave the Judge a copy of the tabloid's interview with Joyce.

At about the same time, Joyce complained that Erik had bad-mouthed her in a television interview with Rona Barrett. So, she asked the Judge to hold Erik in contempt of court as well.

Judge Harry T. Shafer was angry. He met sternly with Erik and Joyce in his chambers for an hour on May 15, 1981 and then marched them into open court. He didn't mince words. "This has been an explosive case," acknowledged the Judge, but "I want this to be the end of it."

He refused to hold either one in contempt for berating the other but warned them it was never to happen again. He ordered that Erik and Joyce were never to mention the other's name, favorably or unfavorably, to any reporter ever again. And, to prevent any recurrence of the fighting between them, the Judge actually ordered that Erik and Joyce never see each other or talk to each other again . . . ever.

Since then, Joyce dated actor John Davidson briefly and then dropped from public view.

CHIPS ended its successful six-year run on NBC in 1983 leaving Erik a millionaire. In 1984, he went on to star as a thoughtful screenwriter in *True West,* a New York play which was not well-received by theatre critics.

Turning down an offer to join the *Falcon Crest* cast as a priest because the role didn't fit his sexy image, Erik spent several months in Italy in 1985 filming a new movie. In it, he portrayed a Mafia hit man in an elaborate expose of organized crime.

But filmmaking was not all that occupied Erik in Italy that year. On August 19, 1985, he married 29-year-old Long Beach, California, model Peggy Rowe in a quiet Catholic ceremony in Rome's St. Paul's Basilica. The 36-year-old groom told reporters that he and Miss Rowe had dated steadily for two years and were ready to settle down and raise a large family.

And how did Estrada get to the church? In a black Mercedes escorted by four Rome motorcycle cops on gleaming bikes who turned out to salute ol' Ponch. The bitter divorce five years before had seen a lot of mud thrown, but his fans were still with him.

Michael Landon, star of "Highway to Heaven" and his wife
Cindy at "An Evening with James Bond" to benefit the
Amanda Foundation at the Playboy Mansion in Los
Angeles. (Scott Downie, Celebrity Photo)

Chapter 13

Michael Landon

For nearly thirty years on television, Michael Landon has exemplified traditional American family values. As Little Joe Cartwright, he was one of three close-knit brothers fiercely loyal to their father. Later, portraying Minnesota homesteader Charles Ingalls, he was the sensitive patriarch of a loving, hard-working frontier family. Today, he's angel Jonathan Smith, who helps people by showing them how to love each other and be kind in their lives.

In his personal life, too, few if any in Hollywood feel more strongly about the importance of the family. In press interviews, when asked what the private Michael Landon is really like, he'll invariably describe himself as a backyard barbecue, play-with-the-kids-in-the-park kind of family man. Actors who have worked with him on his television shows know he stops filming early each day so he can get home to spend the evening with his family.

Without exaggerating it, to millions of his fans and indeed to himself, he's Mr. Family Values. And this is so despite the fact that he's been married three times, had nine kids, sloshed through one quick divorce and one sloppy one, lost custody of his children to his ex-wives and left a wife of eighteen years to marry a blonde beauty twenty years younger than he.

Those contrasts make Landon's story an interesting one, but its real teaching is that in America today a twice divorced person can represent ideal family values in America. That's because the worth of any family is not measured by whether the marital partners stay together. Families of the '80's come in different shapes and forms--single parent households, week-end families and families with step-parents, step-siblings and half-siblings. Some kids need scorecards.

Today's family values don't turn on the form of the family, but rather on the quality of the time spent with the children and the depth of the love they're given. And parents can provide that love for their children and get a divorce for themselves at the same time.

Michael Landon has proved that you don't need custody of your kids to develop strong, loving family bonds with them.

Born Eugene Orowitz in New York in 1936, Landon grew up in working-class Collingswood, New Jersey. The son of warring parents who'd go for weeks refusing to speak to each other in the house, he was the victim of a traumatic childhood. He was belittled for years because of his bed-wetting, often coming home from school to see that his mother had hung his wet sheets out his bedroom window to shame him.

Young Eugene turned to athletics and competed in the javelin throw in high school. The javelin became his life and he spent most of his free time training with it. Developing impressive strength, he broke the national high school javelin record and was the track celebrity of his hometown.

Money was tight in his family and Eugene had to work part-time at a soup factory during high school. It didn't matter that much--he was a terrible student anyway, graduating 300th out of a class of 301. But his javelin arm won him several college track scholarship offers and the javelin was his ticket out of Collingswood.

Excitedly accepting an offer from the University of Southern California in Los Angeles, Gene left years of hurt behind him and moved to the Golden State. During his first year at USC, he tore the ligaments in his arm and was never able to throw the javelin competitively again. Forced off the track team, he left school. But spectacular opportunities abounded for fresh faces in Hollywood and he decided to try his luck.

He figured he needed a new name for his new life and that's how Michael Landon suddenly appeared under Eugene Orowitz's curly mane.

Warner Brothers liked what it saw, enrolled him in their acting school and gave him several bit parts in movies and TV shows. His first starring role was in the 1957 horror flick,

I Was A Teen-Age Werewolf. To Warner's credit, they also assigned him guest appearances on some of their TV westerns.

The young star's sex drive was in high gear, too. In 1955, at nineteen, he married Dodie Fraser, a divorcee with a seven-year-old son. They later adopted another son as well. But the marriage held together only a few years and they divorced just as Landon's star was rising in the West. Over the Ponderosa, that is.

His big break came in 1959 when he was chosen to play Little Joe Cartwright in the *Bonanza* series. Rated the most popular TV show in the country for several years running, its drama and adventure were intensified by the pathos of Ben Cartwright and his sons. Venerable, it continued on the air for fourteen seasons. While Ben, Hoss and Adam did their work at the ranch very seriously, Little Joe tried to have more fun. His character was the romantic lead and the writers had him attempting relationships with several vixen guest stars as they passed through Virginia City.

Michael liked the role so much that even after the cameras stopped filming, he kept a keen eye out for shapely women on the set. Between takes during the shooting of one 1962 episode, he was attracted to Lynn Noe, an amply endowed blonde extra who was wading through the deep mud past a chorus line of horses. Lynn, a former model, was trying to break into show business and the old West never looked better. They fell in love that very first day, made Hop Sing's kitchen steam up during a brief, intense courtship and were married a few months later.

Michael and Lynn remained newlyweds for eighteen years. Publicly affectionate and romantic, they filled their Beverly Hills love nest with five devoted children and made them the center of their universe. Michael explained to interviewers for <u>Nation's Business</u>, "[w]hen I get done at 6 o'clock, I'm done. I go home to my family. I consider my family more important than the job." Lynn thought he was a perfect dad and told the <u>Ladies Home Journal</u> that "no matter how tired Michael is when he gets home, he has time for every one of the children."

Michael tried to teach the kids to be self-reliant, to be fair and honest with others and to work hard in their lives. He imparted those values by being strict with them and not letting them turn into spoiled rich kids. He was an involved and nurturing father.

Since both of them were active in raising the kids, Lynn and Michael had the opportunity to do more things together as parents each year. Their marriage thrived. When an occasional family problem arose, like when their daughter had to be sent to a drug rehabilitation center to live for eighteen months, they looked to each other for the strength and solace needed to cope. They grew stronger as a couple through those ordeals.

In part because of Michael's frequent public effervescence about home and family being the only sources of true happiness and fulfillment, their marriage became the standard in Hollywood to which others were compared.

Bonanza went off the air in 1973, but Michael returned to NBC in prime-time just one year later in *Little House on the Prairie*, another program which relied on family values for its texture. Heartwarming vignettes featured burly frontiersmen and gentle women building their homes and raising their families in the Minnesota of the 1800's. And every night after filming, Michael would rush home to be with his wife and kids.

But while *Little House* enjoyed enormous popularity and was keeping the lights on at NBC during several years when that network's ratings were low, the charcoal in the Landon's backyard grill turned cold. In 1981, Michael filed for divorce. What happened to Hollywood's most famous family man? What was going on at home behind the scenes while Michael was making speeches espousing good, conservative family themes? What gave after eighteen years?

It depends on whom you ask. Lynn will tell you that Michael, at age 44, was going through a mid-life crisis by having a playful affair with the 23-year-old former make-up artist from *Little House.* Yet she expresses no malice for the other woman, Cindy Clerico, because she figures it was just that time in Michael's life and if it hadn't been young Cindy it would have been some other schoolgirl.

When he and Lynn split, Michael moved in with Cindy but vehemently denied that he left Lynn just to be with a younger woman. He was quoted by <u>People</u> magazine as protesting that "you don't dissolve a relationship to go to bed with someone 20 years younger." Instead, he insisted "major differences" had developed between he and Lynn which led to the divorce. As he saw it, they were both unhappy in the marriage and needed out. Still, the divorce hurt. Michael is quick to point out that it's not only the woman who suffers during a divorce--it's every bit as painful for her husband, too.

The next few months went quickly. On December 8, 1981, Judge Billy Mills of the Los Angeles County Superior Court signed a decree dissolving the Landons' marriage. In 1982, *Little House* was cancelled by NBC after eight seasons. Michael married Cindy in 1983. In 1984, *Highway to Heaven* premiered. And, Cindy gave birth to a baby girl in 1983 and a boy in 1986.

Today, Michael is one of the most powerful and successful barons of the entertainment industry. A prominent star who's beloved by millions, he also produces and directs his TV show. He demanded that NBC let him be in charge of every aspect and detail of *Highway* from writing the scripts and hiring the other actors to deciding who sweeps the floor of the sound stage at night. He's one of those people who needs to be in control of everything around him.

But what about those divorces? How do you reconcile being unable to control your wives and families? How do you square being Hollywood's most famous family man and having a divorce record as long as Charles Ingalls' plow?

"Getting a divorce is not losing control" of your life, he argued to <u>TV Guide</u>. You've still got your life; hers is just separate. And as for all those family values, a divorce often will allow you to develop "better relationships" with your children, one-on-one, just you and them. Your bonds with your children are often stronger after a divorce, even if your ex gets custody of them.

The Michael Landon story is a simple one--there can be family after divorce.

Mary Tyler Moore at the 40th Annual Emmy Awards, held at the Pasadena Civic Auditorium. (John Paschal, Celebrity Photo)

Chapter 14

Mary Tyler Moore

On Saturday nights from 1970 to 1977, Mary Tyler Moore "turned the world on with her smile." As Mary Richards, the assistant news producer at WJM-TV in Minneapolis, she symbolized the single career woman of the 1970s. In her thirties and independent, she was the first female star of a modern TV situation comedy who wasn't married or otherwise paired with a man.

Mary Richards was on her own. At the office, we saw her put together the 6:00 p.m. news with Lou Grant, Murray Slaughter, Ted Baxter and Sue Ann Nivens. At home, Rhoda Morgenstern, Georgette Franklin and Phyllis Lindstrom were always popping in. Each week, Mary coped with the challenges of being single and she survived with spunk and verve.

The irony of it all is that it wasn't until her marriage to TV executive Grant Tinker failed in 1979 that she ever experienced for herself the kind of independent life she had lived on television as Mary Richards. The real Mary Tyler Moore had never been anything like Mary Richards and when she finally got the chance at age 42, she really started living.

This All-American girl is an Irish-Catholic from Brooklyn who moved to Southern California with her family when she was eight. Growing up, she was much more interested in her weekly ballet classes than in school and actually became an outstanding dancer.

The day after she graduated from Immaculate Heart High School in Los Angeles in 1955, Mary landed her first job in show business as the Hotpoint Pixie. For Hotpoint appliance ads, she dressed in a little elf-like costume and danced on the top of a stove. A special camera reduced her size down to three inches. Those zippy commercials ran during the popular *Ozzie and Harriet* TV show and young Mary was paid the princely sum of $10,000 a year for doing them.

In high school, she had become rebellious against her strict parents and the Catholic Church. She finally broke with the Church after a Priest told her that prolonged kissing was a mortal sin. To get herself out of her parent's home, she married 27-year-old salesman Richard Meeker when she was 17.

Two months later, she was pregnant and lost her job as the Hotpoint Pixie. Ozzie and Harriet's audience was surely not ready to accept a pregnant pixie dancing on those stoves! A son, Ritchie, was born in 1956. Mary, however, found housework sheer drudgery. She said it was a boring, empty life that would drive her crazy unless she got a job outside the home. At that point, she tried out for the role of Laura Petrie, Dick Van Dyke's TV wife on his promising new show. As Laura, Mary played a very domestic wife who kept the household going for husband Dick while he was at the office writing jokes for the *Allen Brady Show*.

Her own home life was fast losing its luster, though, and she divorced Meeker in February of 1962 after six years of marriage. At the same time, her TV career was booming and she put everything she had into it. The *Dick Van Dyke Show* was a smash with viewers across the country and 24-year-old Mary Tyler Moore was on her way to stardom.

The show turned out to be lucky for Mary in another way as well. Soon after her divorce, she was introduced to handsome advertising executive Grant Tinker one day on the set. It was love at first sight and they were married in Las Vegas on June 1, 1962.

The next 17 years together were golden ones under the California sun. Each of them was enormously successful. Grant earned a reputation for competence in tough jobs at 20th Century Fox, Universal and NBC. In 1970, he formed his own company to produce the new *Mary Tyler Moore Show* for CBS and named it after his wife--MTM Productions. He ran the business smoothly and efficiently. MTM not only broke the bank with that show and its '70s spin-offs, *Rhoda* and *Phyllis*, but it has continued to light up television sets in the '80s with quality hit programs like *Hill Street Blues* and *Newhart*.

During the seven-year run of the *Mary Tyler Moore Show*, Mary became an Emmy-toting superstar. Millions loved her.

At home, the Tinkers were one of Hollywood's most private couples. They didn't even get together socially with the other cast members from the TV series. Mary and Grant kept to themselves in the evenings and on week-ends; and Ed Asner, who played Lou Grant, called them "a closed corporation." But reporters have been able to put together bits and pieces of their very private marriage and a picture is slowly starting to emerge.

They lived in a fabulous $5 million mansion in classy Bel Air. Both wanted a child very much but learned early in their marriage that Mary was diabetic and couldn't bear any more children. However, her son Ritchie lived with them and he was trouble as a child. Growing up in the turbulent 1960s, teen-aged Ritchie ridiculed Mary and Grant's enormous wealth and elegant lifestyle. For a time, he left his mother and moved in with his dad in Fresno.

Grant's four children from his own first marriage often visited, but otherwise few outsiders ever made it past the gates.

Series television is long days and hard work. Mary admits that with her career, she couldn't spend as much time raising Ritchie as she probably should have. Grant bluntly told Ladies Home Journal that he and Mary "feel that we both could have done a better job bringing up the kids."

The personal home life which they coveted was apparently only big enough for the two of them. They were extremely close and deeply attached. Mary told the same magazine interviewer that she was different from so many Hollywood stars who spent their free time espousing various causes. If she did that, she thought she'd be neglecting her main responsibility and her own favorite cause--"the nurturing, care and feeding of a happy marriage."

They basked in each other's companionship and didn't often reach out for other friends. Mary admitted to a Cosmopolitan reporter that "Grant wasn't just my best friend, he was my only friend."

Their days together were usually the same. On weekends, they would lounge around their pool. Fund-raising events for the Diabetes Foundation or infrequent business dinners were about all that would pry them away from their isolated home.

Grant was clearly the dominant partner in the marriage--he made all the major decisions and Mary relied on his instincts. In many ways, he sheltered her. It was sure a far cry from the independence Mary Richards acted out on the CBS set.

In 1977, Mary decided to kill her TV show while it was still on the top of the ratings and in the last episode, a new owner bought WJM and fired everybody but Ted Baxter. The cast scattered--Ed Asner landed his own *Lou Grant* series, Gavin MacLeod signed on as captain of *The Love Boat*, Ted Knight took the lead in *Too Close For Comfort* and Mary went home to Bel Air.

There, she read and considered different movie scripts and offers. In June of that year, she and Grant celebrated their 15th wedding anniversary. Mary busied herself with dance lessons every day and singing lessons three times a week.

But, she increasingly grew edgy and restless. She started seeing an analyst, chain-smoked 2 1/2 packs of cigarettes a day and coped with her boredom by doing crossword puzzles for hours at a time and needlepoint until her fingers hurt. In fact, she went so wild with it that she needlepointed 23 giant pillows in four years.

In February, 1978, Mary was staggered by the strange death of her younger sister, Elizabeth. A college student who also worked in the news department of a local TV station, Elizabeth became distraught when her boyfriend dumped her. Heartbroken, she was sedating herself with Darvon. One night, she took 20 or 25 of them, which really shouldn't have killed her, but something in her system reacted adversely and she was gone. Her death was a terrible blow to Mary.

In 1978 and 1979, Mary and Grant's marriage began to sputter. No one knew about it at the time, though, because that would be the last thing the press would get out of the town's most secluded twosome. In fact, in press interviews at the time, they both acted as if everything was perfect. Grant raved about how surprising it was that a superstar of Mary's caliber could be so natural and homespun. For her part, Mary criticized other Hollywood celebrities who aired their dirty linen in the press. She complained that too many family secrets were spilled which the public didn't need to know, and vowed to do everything in her power to keep her own private life private. And for good reason particularly at that time--her marriage was teetering on the brink.

Grant and Mary talked for days about how the sands had shifted in their relationship. They realized it was over; and without bitterness or anger, they decided to separate in the fall of 1979. Neither felt the need right then to formally file for divorce, so Mary simply moved directly to New York City to start a new life.

The movie *Ordinary People* premiered in 1980 to rave reviews from critics and immense public popularity. Donald Sutherland played wealthy Chicago tax attorney Calvin Jarrett. Timothy Hutton was the high school student son, Conrad, who had been treated at a psychiatric hospital following an unsuccessful suicide attempt. Mary won an Academy Award nomination for her portrayal of Beth, the cold mother who blamed Conrad for the death of his brother, who was Beth's favorite.

It was an emotional film that made people cry. Mary would later admit to reporters that she drew on her own strained relationship with her son, Ritchie, when playing Beth. She knew how to act out distance and reserve between a mother and her son because she'd already lived it in her own life.

In October, 1980, Mary got an urgent phone call from Grant in California. The news was virtually unbearable--24-year-old Ritchie had accidentally killed himself with a shotgun. His housemate had asked him about his girlfriend and Ritchie put the gun to his head and pulled the trigger, saying "she loves me, she loves me not," and it suddenly fired.

Those with him at the time insisted it was accidental and not a suicide.

Mary went through hell. Her only child was dead before she had time to fully rebuild their relationship. Even though they had not been close during his teens, they were in the process of reconciling; and Ritchie was warming to her as he grew older. Mary was looking forward to a new life with him and then, suddenly, in a shotgun blast, it was over.

Words can't capture the pain a mother feels for the death of her child; and 1980 had brought not only Ritchie's death but Mary's separation from the husband to whom she'd been riveted for 17 years. It was devastating and traumatic, but she kept plugging on with her life. She admitted finding it difficult to maintain her belief in God after all that had happened to her. Friends knew she couldn't call on religion for much comfort from her sense of pain and loss.

After living apart for a year, the Tinkers decided it would be best for each of them if they sought a divorce. Mary filed a petition for dissolution of marriage in the Los Angeles County Superior Court on December 30, 1980, citing irreconcilable differences as the reason. Using her legal name of Mary M. Tinker to sign the petition, she also requested that the judge restore her former name, Mary Tyler Moore.

Grant did not contest the divorce, but allowed it to sail smoothly through the Los Angeles court system. Easily one of the most civilized Hollywood divorces, it was refreshingly free of rancor and hostility. Mary and Grant sat down and agreed to divide their property evenly between them. Mary got one-half of the shares of MTM Enterprises, the mansion at 760 Lausanne Road in Bel Air, the home's furniture and artwork, her profits from *Ordinary People,* the full ownership of their Screen Actors Guild pension and $1,116,147 in cold cash.

Grant's half of their assets included 1,500 shares of stock in CBS, 1,600 shares of ABC and 1,000 shares of NBC; their second home located at 2680 Deep Canyon Road in Beverly Hills, the right to buy the Bel Air mansion if Mary ever decided to sell it, $400,000 in MTM Enterprises accounts receivable, $750,000 in accounts receivable from Company Four--another business which he and Mary owned, his personal IRA, their 1979 tax refund, $1,000 in U.S. Savings Bonds and their membership in the Bel Air Country Club.

In other clauses of the agreement, Mary promised to repay a $978,000 officer's loan she had taken out from MTM Enterprises and both agreed to split the attorneys' fees for the divorce 50-50.

On April 15, 1981 Judge William Hogoboom reviewed the 15-page settlement agreement and found it to be fair. He approved it and granted an interlocutory decree of divorce which restored Mary's former name. The final judgment of divorce was entered on June 11, 1982.

It was one of the cleanest breaks in Hollywood history. Mary told reporters afterward that while the divorce was not easy on her, she and Grant had remained close friends and talked on the phone regularly since their marriage ended.

Grant, the ultimate TV producer, stoically drew an industry analogy for Cosmopolitan magazine: "Relationships wear out and come to an end, just like shows."

Mary started a fresh new life in New York City and admits relying on the old *Mary Tyler Moore* Show scripts as her roadmaps through the unexplored territory of single life. She remembered how Mary Richards handled being on her own; and she started doing at age 42 what most young women do at 22--having fun, reaching out for new experiences, experimenting with life and doing what she herself wanted to do. She was free to pursue her own interests--not restricted to those of her husband. Now, after being married continuously and working like a dog since graduating from high school 25 years before, she was alone and on her own for the first time.

She was off . . . and living. Mary went skiing for the first time in her life, took up horseback riding, bought a golden retriever ("Dash") and entered him in dog shows. She went to parties alone and began meeting a variety of new and exciting people from other fields who were emotionally and intellectually stimulating. She made friends with artists, novelists, painters, photographers and Broadway theatre stars.

Mary wanted to put California behind her, so she sold the Bel Air home to Grant and left nearly all of her furniture and possessions behind. She moved into an elegant apartment in New York overlooking a lake in Central Park and decorated it with modern snow white furniture and South American artifacts.

Her typical day in New York was to wake up between 9:00 and 10:30 a.m.; go to a ballet lesson or dance class; meet someone for a business lunch, for instance to review a script; in the afternoon, attend a session with a tutor in one of her new interests like political science; meet with her analyst three times a week for consultation and finish the day by answering her fan mail in her apartment. She usually had dinner with friends.

She stuffed herself with greasy cheeseburgers and french fries and washed it all down with six Tabs a day.

She even changed her politics when she moved to New York. A lifelong Republican, she opposed Ronald Reagan in 1980 and actually made a TV commercial for Jimmy Carter.

In contrast to her predictable, housebound life in California, she was on the move every day in New York. Mary began walking everywhere and, like a kid, was excited by all the new things she was seeing in America's largest city. She thought about her metamorphosis for a _Time_ magazine reporter and concluded, "I really am a late bloomer when you stop to think about it."

Two and a half years after moving to New York, Mary fell in love with a handsome young doctor. The scene was the emergency room of Mt. Sinai Hospital, where Mary had taken her mother for tests in October of 1982. Mary was struck by the tenderness and compassion of Robert Levine, the medical resident on duty who comforted her mother.

On Mary's next visit to the hospital, Dr. Levine showed concern for the star's health as well. He noted that Mary was quite pale and asked if she was ill. She explained that she was a diabetic and that it had been an "off day" for her.

He told her to call him in any emergency at any hour of the day or night if she had any problems controlling her diabetes. She asked him if loneliness was a sufficient medical emergency for her to call. Beaming, he said he couldn't think of a better reason.

Within a few days, Mary summoned the courage to telephone him at 2:00 a.m. one morning and ask him out for dinner. They went the next night and hit it off spectacularly. There were fireworks and Mary knew she had found a fresh love for her new life. Within a few months, they began living together.

They were married on November 23, 1983 in a traditional Jewish ceremony at New York's posh Hotel Pierre in front of 300 guests from show business and the medical profession. They were a study in contrasts--he was Jewish, she was raised Catholic. He was an unknown cardiologist whose friends were mostly yuppie doctors fresh out of med school, she was a national television celebrity who had lived her entire adult life in Tinsel Town and moved in the circles of the rich and famous. But the most startling contrast was their ages--she was 45, he was 30.

Mary had robbed the cradle and that 16-year age difference was the big story of their wedding. When the press told her that her fans were concerned about it, Mary told them not to worry, that everything was fine. She explained that rather than how old he was, the important things to her were that she and Robert shared the same values and that he was secure, successful in his own right and funny.

The public's reaction to the spring-autumn romance was mixed. Many women saw Mary as a trailblazer whose decision to marry somebody so much younger than she would encourage other older women to do the same.

But some of her own friends were skeptical. People magazine quoted one of them as confiding that Robert was, in person and up close, "a big bore who's never been around or done anything interesting." On top of that, according to this account, he talks about medicine all the time and is ugly when you get a good look. Some described him as just a "nerd."

But Mary loves him and that's probably all that counts. And with him, she has started living a much different life.

Robert turned her into a toucher and a hugger. He's so extremely sensitive that Mary has been able to turn to him with her problems and anxieties just like she would her analyst. He has been a gentle stream of comfort to her.

During the first year of their marriage, Mary made headlines when she checked into the Betty Ford Center in Rancho Mirage, California, for treatment of an alcohol problem. Robert was quick to point out to the press that Mary was not an alcoholic, but she was at the detox center because her social drinking was increasingly dangerous to her diabetes. He explained that her evening cocktails upset her body's insulin-fed chemical balance. Her treatment was successful.

By the winter of 1985, Mary had quit smoking, too, and started chewing gum instead. She takes ballet lessons twice a week and pushes herself to get as much exercise as possible to help control her diabetes.

On December 11, 1985, she returned to television in a new situation comedy, *Mary,* and in it played a columnist for a Chicago tabloid. The show, however, flopped after just 13 episodes. She attempted to bounce back three years later as a New York City community relations coordinator in *Annie McGuire*, a new CBS comedy which also sputtered in the ratings and headed straight for the video boneyard.

How has she coped? After all of that personal pain, how can she still smile so broadly and do comedy on TV for a living in front of millions? Mary has forged a philosophy of life. First, no one's life is entirely happy--pain strikes everyone. Second, nothing lasts forever, so don't expect it to. Third, accept that there are some things that will happen in your life over which you have no control. Fourth, pain, unpleasant and unbearable as it is, will force you to reach the heights of courage and bravery in your life as you overcome it.

Mary has admitted that at times her grief has been unbearable and that she has cried for hours. But she has reminded herself that others have it a lot worse.

From all of these personal tragedies, Mary has emerged confident, composed and strong. She is going to make it after all.

Winning smiles of John and Rita Jenrette. (Photo: Bill Scroggins)

Chapter 15

John and Rita Jenrette

The Jenrette divorce is a story of skin and scam--the gorgeous, sultry young wife posing nude for <u>Playboy</u> to raise money for her husband's appeal from an Abscam bribery conviction, only to learn he was seeing another woman on the sly.

It's a saga that goes behind closed doors in Washington, D.C. to the party circuit of the politically powerful and their wild, raucous boozing. It goes behind the stately columns of the United States Capitol where Congressman Jenrette and his wife openly fornicated one night during a late evening House session, and to the yachts and mansions of rich politicians where extramarital flings and seductions were but an evening's entertainment. And this story, finally, goes behind prison bars at the federal pen in Atlanta where John Jenrette landed after a frenzied tailspin caused by his insatiable appetite for money, alcohol and sex.

They met outside the United States Capitol building in 1976 when John's alert, wandering eye spotted the 26-year-old former Texas beauty queen. She was standing there, absolutely luminous and looking like a covergirl model fresh from the pages of some glamour magazine. It was simply too much temptation for John. He introduced himself to her as a Capitol elevator operator and asked if she'd enjoy a ride. Once inside the building, though, he went straight to the "Members Only" elevator and squired her up to his office, admitting that in fact he was the freshman Congressman from South Carolina.

But as he stood talking with this blonde vixen, a new sewer system for Horry County was the furthest thing from his mind. Said the gentleman spider to the fly, why don't you jet to the Virgin Islands with me tonight and we'll play in the nude on the beach all day tomorrow? No, she already had a date that night. Not a problem, said he, "I do too."

They did start going together, however, and were married a few months later by a justice of the peace in historic Alexandria. The ceremony was marred by John's beeper going off before they could say "I do," and he was rushed back to the Capitol for an important role call vote. Five hours later, he was on a plane flying to South Carolina to make several appearances and speeches in his re-election campaign. Rita spent her wedding night alone in their small apartment.

John was a love machine, though, and once he put out the political fires back in his district, he came home eager to redeem himself. At 10:00 p.m. one night that week while the House was in late-night session, John slipped out the back door and met Rita in the shadows of the building's huge marble columns. The rush of sex in a public place overcame them and they wildly rutted right there on the Capitol steps, wrapped in Rita's fur coat. Tip O'Neill went by and waved to John. John giggled.

While impulsive, uncontrollable sex would fuel their marriage in the express lane, the urge was so overpowering in John that he reportedly couldn't resist new conquests. According to Rita, after they'd been married just one year and were on vacation at the beach, she went looking for John at 4:00 a.m. one morning when he didn't return to bed. She found the little devil in a storeroom naked as a jaybird in the arms of a woman, similarly unclad, who Rita figured was old enough to be her mother. Rita went wild with rage. She knocked out the window panes with her bare hands, threw her clothes in her suitcase and caught the first morning flight back to Washington.

She was met at the airport by some of John's aides who were there to protect the Congressman from any embarrassing publicity. As they talked, Rita cooled down and they agreed to work together to try to save John from the bottle. She didn't want his drinking problem to ruin their young marriage and the staffers didn't want it to cost John his seat in Congress.

Washington, D.C., however, is no place for a Congressman to dry out. Tempted by endless parties, receptions and dinners at which the liquor flowed freely, John kept his lips to the shot glass. And the more he drank, according to Rita, the more womanizing he did.

The airlines were John's link to his district and one more cash bar in his life. He'd often start drinking as soon as he'd get on a plane. At 28,000 feet and 80 proof, people who saw it say he'd openly flirt with and pinch the stewardesses. Rita remembered ten or twenty trips when he was so skunk drunk by the time the flight landed in South Carolina that she'd have to put him to bed. Then, she'd make his speeches for him, telling audiences that he was delayed in Washington on urgent business and couldn't be there as planned.

It got so bad that Rita forced him to seek treatment at the Schick Alcoholism Center in Dallas, but when she paid a surprise visit a few days later she caught him playing around with one of the nurses. Rita was livid and told John he should just paint a penis on his pants so every woman would know he was easy. On top of that, she discovered that when he registered, he told the doctors he was there to be disabused of his thirst for Scotch when in truth he was a two-fisted Brandy drinker. He never did like Scotch.

The bottle spoiled their 1979 Christmas, too. After she waited all night for John to come home for a family Christmas Eve dinner, he stumbled in at dawn not even knowing what day it was.

Six weeks later, the FBI stunned Congress by announcing it had arrested one Senator and six House members on bribery charges. Each had allegedly taken $50,000 in cash from federal agents posing as wealthy Arab sheiks who were seeking to buy political influence. The guts of the government's case was hidden-camera video tapes which caught the Congressmen right in the act in hotel suites and town houses in the nation's capital. Abscam was the name of the program and Congressman John W. Jenrette, Jr. of South Carolina was one of its stars.

Embarrassing as Abscam was for the Congress, it actually drew John and Rita closer. The criminal charges and threat that he could be sent to a federal pen for 35 years scared John into finally seriously seeking treatment for his alcoholism. He entered the U.S. Naval Hospital in Bethesda in early 1980 and there were early signs that some progress was being made. Rita stood by him.

In September of that year, John went on trial and, attempting to explain away the FBI's video tapes, contended that he had simply been too drunk to know what he was doing when he took the bait from the undercover agents. The jury didn't buy it and found him guilty. He immediately vowed to appeal the conviction.

The voters of South Carolina turned him out of office two months later, and the responsibility for raising the money to finance John's appeal fell to Rita. She put her talents to work writing an expose of her years as the wife of a congressman, years she said she hated. Prominently published in the Washington Post a few weeks later, her behind-the-scenes revelations jolted official Washington and unofficial Myrtle Beach. Putting down many of John's South Carolina supporters as "double-knit suited alligator shoe boys" who'd kiss their wives good-bye supposedly for a week-end of fishing only to shack up with their mistresses for some cheap sex, Rita wrote that at least she wouldn't have to pretend to like those people anymore. She labeled his constituents as dumb and cheap.

John's cronies back home in South Carolina were furious and Rita became the easy target of an angry local groundswell. Radio station WNMB even played a new song, "Ode to Rita," which featured this refrain: "You think you're so pretty and you think you've got so much class ... but, Rita, you ain't nothin' but a pain in the ass."

Her lurid article also chronicled John's blatant womanizing and sloppy boozing, but Rita was willing to forgive his past indiscretions and stand loyally by him in his time of need. She even pledged to sell the house, the Mercedes and the fur coat made famous on the Capitol steps to finance his appeal.

Fast becoming a national celebrity in her own right, Rita next consented to an in-depth Playboy magazine interview and nude photo spread. Playboy paid big money for interviews and even more for accompanying skin, so Rita spilled her guts and showed them, too. In the interview, she spoke of the sexual promiscuity of leading politicians. An example she provided involved her week-end on a governor's yacht where the Gov felt up her leg while she was napping on a deck chair and later walked in on her while she was taking a shower.

Her literary appetite whetted, she penned a steamy book, *My Capitol Secrets*, revealing more intimate details of the rocky marriage to her gentleman from South Carolina.

The sole source of their financial support as John quarterbacked his appeal, Rita found quick money and enthusiastic receptions on the lecture and talk show circuit. No question about it, people were anxious to hear more about her tantalizing escapades set against the backdrop of Washington sex and politics.

After several weeks of these public appearances, she returned home in January, 1981, for a few days off. John had run to Miami, leaving only a telephone number. When Rita tried contacting him, she learned the number was phony, and she knew at once that he had fled to be with one of his old girlfriends who lived there. Frantically rummaging through his closet, her heart stopped . . . there, bulging from one of his brown suede shoes were thousands of dollars in $100 bills. That wasn't his unemployment check--as the serial numbers later confirmed, that was marked Abscam bribery money he'd been hiding all along.

Finding that money was the final straw for Rita. In defeat, she told reporters for the Columbia, S.C., morning newspaper, The State: "I stuck with him as long as I can. I've endured enough. I can't take it any more." Within days, she filed for a legal separation, charging in her complaint that John "has committed numerous acts of cruelty . . . and has held [me] to ridicule and scorn." She argued that John's adulterous snaking behind her back had made the marriage "intolerable" and caused her "to suffer great mental and physical injury and anguish." She demanded alimony from John and half of all their assets.

Her divorce would go nowhere, though, as long as John remained in Miami where he couldn't be personally served with the papers. Rita and her attorneys quietly laid in wait, and when John jaunted off the elevator on the sixth floor of the Federal courthouse in Washington at 10:00 a.m. on February 10, 1981, to appear before Judge John G. Penn for his Abscam appeal, a U.S. Marshall slapped Rita's divorce papers in his hand. Color him served.

Unamused, John's attorneys objected and called it "a cheap publicity trick." To the horde of reporters who were also waiting for John to arrive that morning on Abscam business and who were treated to a second case as well, John laughed that Rita was charging him with numerous acts of cruelty. He quipped, "I scratched her when I was putting on the fur coat."

John filed an answer to Rita's divorce petition a few weeks later and agreed the marriage should be dissolved. But, he stunned her by arguing to the Court that because Rita was now raking in big money as an author and media celebrity, she should pay him alimony. After all, the purpose of alimony was to maintain the divorced spouse in the standard of living to which they'd become accustomed during the marriage and it was John who in this case was unemployed and flat on his back financially.

John's lawyers going in tough on alimony forced Rita to compromise and quickly agree to an out-of-court settlement. The major asset of the marriage, a home at 160 N. Carolina Avenue in Washington which John had bought in 1977, was ordered sold and the proceeds of the sale divided 50-50.

On July 21, 1981, Judge Nicholas S. Nunzio of the District of Columbia Superior Court heard the case and issued a formal order. He dissolved the marriage, approved their agreement to sell the house and divide the proceeds, awarded the Mercedes to Rita and ruled that neither one was entitled to alimony from the other. Recognizing the bitterness, hard feelings and hatred both John and Rita had for each other, the Judge also ordered that "neither shall in any manner whatsoever molest or trouble the other."

Once the best known couple in Washington, they went their separate ways . . . Rita to starring in TV and movies and John to prison.

Unsuccessful in appealing his bribery conviction, John made a last-ditch plea for leniency in 1983 to avoid hard time by telling the Judge he was willing to stay out of jail to do his part to ease any "further burden [on] the overcrowded prisons." The Judge scoffed at John's transparent civic-mindedness and with steel in his voice sentenced him to two years incarceration in the federal penitentiary in Atlanta. John also was hit with a $20,000 fine. After buying himself several months of freedom with further legal delays, John reported to prison in April, 1985, and was taken into custody.

John had turned irascible in dealing with Rita in the months before he entered the pen. He also felt the FBI was watching everything he did. Boxed in, he refused to sign the deed so the Washington townhouse they owned could be sold as the divorce Judge ordered. It was John's fear that the federal government would immediately attach his share of the profits and apply it to the $20,000 in Abscam fines unpaid by him and the tens of thousands of dollars given John by the FBI undercover agents which was still unaccounted for. He figured the government would get all of his share of the house and he was just fiesty enough to try to keep them from it.

But a few months behind bars took the fight out of him and in August he agreed to Rita's demands and she was able to get her money out of the house and wash her hands of him.

John, for his part, went about the business of being a model prisoner. He was released thirteen months later, in May of 1986, and detailed to a halfway house in Florence, South Carolina. One of the first things he did as a free man was to attend a gala Democratic political rally in Galivants Ferry, where he was greeted enthusiastically by former campaign workers and friends who hugged him and cheered his release from prison. Today, he heads the John Jenrette Center for the Children of Alcoholics and spends his time counselling young people to steer clear of the booze that cost him his career.

Rita, ever the buxom beauty, is trying to cash in on her striking looks and household centerfold name as an actress. She made her television debut in a 1982 episode of *Fantasy Island*, to yawning silence on the part of most critics. Striking out on TV, she switched to movies and starred as a victim in the 1987 horror film, *Zombie Island Massacre*. In it, she played the last surviving tourist on a sightseeing bus whose passengers were being mysteriously killed one-by-one.

Not only did Rita win flattering reviews, that role was the perfect one to launch her film career. Because, in real life, through all the glitter and then the ghoul of her Washington whirl, she was married to a lying, cheating zombie and she survived it. She looks back on it philosophically: "I'm not proud of the pain and the punishment I endured, but I will say that it has made me a stronger woman today." Rita 2, Zombies 0.

Singer Anita Bryant at a press conference in Miami Beach, Florida, explaining that her prospective TV show had been cancelled by a sponsor because of her stand against gay rights. (AP Wirephoto, Wide World Photos, Inc.)

Chapter 16

Anita Bryant

It took a painful divorce in 1980 to make Anita Bryant a true Christian. A popular singer and television star, she became the nation's best known anti-gay rights crusader in the 1970s. She even established an evangelical ministry dedicated to preserving the American family. Her own shocking 1980 divorce, regarded as an unforgivable sin by her fellow fundamentalists, caused many of her right-wing Christian followers to reject and revile her.

When the Florida Citrus Commission fired her as its $100,000 a year spokeswoman because of her divorce, a stung Anita told reporters she now knew what it felt like to be persecuted. After she thought about it a few days, she announced that she could understand for the first time the anger and frustration felt by gays and feminists when they were discriminated against. Her own divorce transformed her from hate-filled militant to forgiving shepherd; and today Anita preaches that gays should be treated like human beings, with love and understanding.

The inside story of her divorce rivals the 1987 PTL Club scandal in evangelical intrigue. It all began in 1958 when young Anita, the daughter of a part-Indian roustabout from the Oklahoma oil fields, competed in the Miss America Pageant to earn money for college. Singing in the talent competition, she brought the house down and was voted second runner-up. She enrolled at Northwestern University with her prize money. But that same year, she was asked to cut a record ("Till There Was You") and it sold a million copies before her classes even started. Overnight, she became one of the country's top new recording stars. And instead of going to college, she began dating Bob Green, Miami's number one disc jockey.

Bob, nine years older than Anita, was a dashing Miami celebrity. He was strikingly handsome and always surrounded by beautiful women. He drove a white Thunderbird with his name on the side and was known wherever he went in town. Anita called him a "dreamboat."

How they met and why they were attracted to each other is a prime example of cupid's arrow being dipped in physical attraction rather than loftier values and shared church philosophy. Anita, intensely religious since her childhood in the Oklahoma Bible belt, was engaged to Pat Boone's brother, Nick. She, Pat and Shirley Boone went off to Miami during that time to plug their records at a convention of disc jockeys. When Anita spotted the dazzling Green, Pat Boone's brother was history.

After dating and planning their June 25, 1960 wedding for a year, Anita came close to backing out at the last minute. The more she thought about it, she had doubts about Bob's religious convictions. She had accepted Christ when she was 8 years old and had assiduously lived the conservative life of a born-again Christian. Was this handsome guy really devout enough or was he one of the devil's temptations? She confronted Bob and told him she didn't think she could go through with the ceremony. Then, the day before the wedding, Bob and Anita prayed together and he confessed Jesus Christ as his Lord and Savior. The wedding went on as scheduled.

They chose Miami as their home and soon moved into a $300,000 Spanish-style mansion on the Atlantic Ocean. Bob gave up his radio career and became Anita's full-time manager. Keeping with her religious image, he didn't book her into nightclubs. Instead, she took her act to state fairs and conventions all across the country.

Her singing career boomed during the 1960s and 1970s with her "Paper Roses" and "My Little Corner Of The World" records selling millions. She appeared on TV commercials for Kraft Foods and was the Coca-Cola Girl long before Bill Cosby ever snuggled up to a can of Coke or Michael Jackson ever styled around a Pepsi.

Anita belted out stirring patriotic songs on USO shows with Bob Hope and touched millions singing on televised Billy Graham Crusades. Her theme song was a gripping rendition of "The Battle Hymn of the Republic" and she was in such demand nationally that in 1968 she sang at both the

Republican and Democratic National Conventions. She even sang at President Lyndon Johnson's funeral in 1973.

Smiling and chirping under the Florida sunshine tree, Anita splashed rivers of orange juice over her golden vocal chords as the national spokeswoman for the Florida Citrus Commission from 1968 to 1980. She made 76 different television commercials in the orange juice job and was paid $100,000 a year. Her cash register would also ring up $7,500 for each of her 40 appearances at conventions and annual corporate meetings each year. A lot of that must've gone into the collection plate at the ultra-conservative Northwest Baptist Church in Miami because the Bryants' whole lives revolved around religion.

They raised a family of four cheerful kids whose ages by 1980 were sixteen, fifteen and twins who were ten. Strictly disciplined, the children participated fully in their parents' religious activities. When they would get out of line, Bob never hesitated to spank them even as they grew older.

Anita taught Sunday School and Bob was a deacon in the church. She has written eight books about religion, and the theme of every one of them is to trust God's word as revealed in the Bible and put your life in His hands. He'll take care of your career and your life. She sincerely believes Jesus speaks directly to her and that He makes tough decisions for her.

From all appearances, the Bryants lived a devout Christian home life. They had a prayer altar built right into their 27-room shanty and Bob must've really liked what he heard there. The Bible taught Anita that it was God's will that she submit to Bob. The man was the head of the household and the woman was to be totally submissive to him. Anita followed that order to the letter and it ruled her life. It also ruined her marriage and made every year of it a living hell for her.

A stormy marriage raged behind their born again smiles. Anita told Ladies Home Journal reporters in 1980 that Bob really hated her all those years. She explained that he gave her "no respect, no trust, no affection, no love life, no recognition as a worthwhile human being." He was jealous of most of the hundreds of men she would meet professionally, and he would accuse her of being sexually attracted to strangers. Behind the scenes, they fought all the time and they degraded each other even in public. She admitted having no feeling for him at all after five years of marriage and holding on for the next fifteen years only because of her religion. She truly believed it was a wife's lot to submit to her husband and accept anything he dished out.

It was a tough road for Anita and she sought the help of numerous marriage counselors along the way. She resorted to dangerously increasing dosages of Valium and sleeping pills to cope. Toward the end of the marriage, she actually became quite ill, plagued by severe headaches, chest pains, muscle spasms and depression.

Bob manipulated her and controlled her life. As her manager, he booked her into more and more engagements and kept intense career pressure on her every day. She was worn down to a nub.

Bob became a religious fanatic and he forced her to dramatically increase her public witnessing. In fact, he is the one who harassed her into leading the 1977 fight in Miami to repeal the city's new laws that protected homosexuals from employment and housing discrimination. Anita, sheltered as she was, didn't even know that much about it. She disclosed to Playboy interviewers that Bob's the one who taught her about homosexuality: "He is nine years older and he has taught me a lot of things about sex." She admitted that Bob had to explain to her what two men could do in a bed: "I didn't really know the nitty-gritty of the thing."

Anita told friends she was opposed to getting involved in the gay controversy. But, Bob ordered her to battle the gays and told her to pray about it to see what God wanted her to do. Sure enough, Anita became convinced that she was being tapped by God to lead the fight against the homosexuals.

She became the nation's most outspoken anti-gay crusader and spearheaded the Miami grassroots campaign to roll back those gay ordinances. Her theme was to "Save Our Children" from homosexual teachers as role models and from other homosexual influences.

When making speeches, she would say that "if God had condoned homosexuality, He would have placed Adam and Bruce in the Garden of Eden." She recruited 3,000 volunteers to go door-to-door spreading the word against the gays. Miami's voters enthusiastically rallied around her and, in the referendum, voted two-to-one to repeal the gay laws.

The behind-the-scenes driving force, Bob rushed into the limelight on election night at the victory party. With television cameras fixed on Anita, he ran up and gave her a big kiss, saying, "This is what heterosexuals do, fellows."

During the next few months Anita kissed a banana cream pie, pressed into her face by an irate opponent, and she became the object of hatred and ridicule swelling within gays across the country. She received death threats so serious that her home was fortified like a bunker, and she was connected to a beeper hooked up to police headquarters which could bring the cops running in 30 seconds. All her mail was delivered three days late so it could first be X-rayed for bombs.

But the gays didn't try to blow her away after all. What they did do was to picket her wherever she performed. That got results. Not one single corporation booked her for a convention that year because they didn't want the controversy; and Anita lost an estimated $350,000 convention income. Many gays attempted to organize a boycott of Florida orange juice but the Citrus Commission loyally stood by its spokeswoman and refused to fire her.

As she weathered the bitter controversy which engulfed her career, she was voted the most admired woman in America by readers of Good Housekeeping magazine for two years in a row for standing up for what she believed was right. She paid a price--the backlash to her anti-gay campaign ruined her career.

She formed Anita Bryant Ministries to carry on the fundamentalists' fight to preserve the traditional American family. The idea was that things like homosexuality, atheism and divorce threatened families and somebody needed to keep those evils in check. Bob was named President of the organization and took charge of its day-to-day operations. But slowly, he began to squeeze Anita out of the decisions and run the show himself. The more powerful Bob became at the Ministries, the more he demanded Anita be submissive to him in every facet of their lives. Their marriage was being strained to the limit.

In a funny yet perceptive article, <u>Playboy</u> reported Anita's marriage difficulties to its readers by explaining that Satan "eggs her on to kick Bob's ass when Bob does something dumb," but that her born-again side commands her to be submissive to him.

Desperately, Bob and Anita finally reached out for the help of a conservative Christian marriage counselor, B. Larry Coy. Coy's advice to Anita: God has said that the man is head of the house. Obey him.

Bob started coming down hard on Anita for her awakening rebelliousness as she began to question the rightness of Coy's advice and the church's marital philosophy. At a meeting of the Board of Directors of the Anita Bryant Ministries, Anita was humiliated in public when charged with unfaithfulness to church doctrine because she was starting to believe she shouldn't have to be Bob's slave in their marriage. They even threatened to discipline her if she didn't repent and change her ways fast.

Bob and those good old boys running the business obviously figured using the church in that way would force Anita to stay in the marriage. But they misjudged the spunky 5'2" scrapper. Anita got up from her chair, glowered meanly at Bob for several moments, cracked "good luck with the Bob Green Ministries" and walked right out the door.

Now convinced Bob wasn't worthy of her, she filed for divorce on May 22, 1980.

Within a month, Bob filed a response with the court asking that Anita's petition not be acted on. Bob told the Judge that the marriage could be preserved if he and Anita had spiritual counseling and more time to work it out. His court papers contained several Biblical verses and references to God being able to save this Christian marriage.

Anita just couldn't believe it. She fired back a blunt and crackling answer to set the Judge straight about all of Bob's mumbo jumbo. She laid it on the line--for several years they had been seeing marriage counselors, psychiatrists and church leaders because they fought like cats and dogs. They were incompatible and despite all that counseling no one had been successful in holding the marriage together. Anita told the Associated Press that the bottom line was that the marriage "wasn't all that great to begin with." So, to Bob's request that the divorce proceedings be indefinitely postponed so God could go to work on it, Anita said kiss off. She asked the Judge to get his pen out and free her from Bob Green.

It didn't take long. By August 15, Judge Murray Goldman had heard enough. Sitting at his desk in his Miami courthouse office, he quietly signed a one-page order dissolving the Greens' marriage. His decree approved and incorporated a lengthy agreement hammered out between Bob's and Anita's attorneys concerning all the details.

Custody of the 10-year old twins was awarded to Anita. Bob was given liberal visitation rights, including one month each summer, every other week-end and the right to take them to dinner one night each week. The two older children could choose with whom they would live. (Later, the 16-year old boy decided to go with Bob and the 15-year old girl stayed with Anita)

Bob was ordered to pay $200 a month per child as child support and retain Anita and the kids as irrevocable beneficiaries on his life insurance. Their waterfront villa was to be sold and the profits divided 50-50. Anita was given the Mercedes and Ford van; Bob kept the Thunderbird and Cadillac.

The transformation in Anita Bryant's life after her divorce ranks as one of the most extreme ever to occur. Her fundamentalist followers turned on her and she had to cancel all religious concerts. To born-again Christians, she had failed in her marriage and, therefore, simply didn't have a religious message anymore. So, they didn't want her at their gatherings. She was a fallen angel, a sinner no longer pure and perfect enough. For years, she had been on the front lines for the fundamentalists, fighting for their controversial causes and taking a lot of personal abuse for it. Now, when the time came in her own life when she needed support, they treated her like poor relation. It must have broken her heart.

She disassociated herself from Anita Bryant Ministries, figuring you can't have a celebrated divorcee heading an organization whose purpose it is to preserve the family unit.

The Florida Citrus Commission fired her as its national spokeswoman because of the divorce; and she fled to Selma, Alabama, to live in seclusion with her children. With so few people asking her to perform anymore, she opened a dress shop to make money.

She was on her back. And from that perspective, she did a lot of thinking about her church and her life. About leading that virulent and strident campaign against homosexuals? "The answers don't seem so simple now," she reflected for the Ladies Home Journal. About that church doctrine that a woman must be submissive to her husband? "Fundamentalists have their head in the sand," she snapped. About being branded as a sinner and shunned by the born-agains after her divorce? "The church needs to wake up and find some way to cope with divorce and women's problems."

And how is Bob Green taking all of this after the divorce? What divorce? he asks. His fundamentalist religious beliefs don't recognize civil divorce proceedings, and he says that in God's eyes Anita is still his wife. The wedding ring stayed on his finger. He changed the name of Anita Bryant Ministries to Crusade For Morality and dedicated himself to continuing the vigorous fight against homosexuals everywhere.

While Bob is back to bashing gays, Anita now condemns the ignorance of the fundamentalists that would breed such hate. She remains a devout Christian, but her divorce has tempered her to moderation. She doesn't apologize for her opposition to the gay rights ordinances, yet espouses a "live and let live" philosophy today.

She faded from public view during her years in Selma and quietly moved to Atlanta in 1984. By 1988, her hurt had healed to the point that she thought she could face the public again and return to entertaining. She launched a gutsy comeback and recorded *Anita With Love*, a brand new album of gospel songs and music from the big band era.

Guest hosting *The 700 Club*, she made it known to the country that her years of exile were over. Later in 1988, she went back on the road for the first time in ten years with a new concert act. Appearing at small town fairs and Elks Clubs across the South, she delivers her "Battle Hymn of the Republic" and "Paper Roses" trademarks with the feeling and flair of the old Anita. It is good to see her again.

From saint to sinner in one jump is traumatic, but Anita has made her fall from the evangelists' pedestal a graceful one. She clings to God, takes one day at a time and believes that in the long run, God will vindicate her decision to divorce Bob. She assures friends, "I will survive--I'm unsinkable."

Clint Eastwood attending the premiere of "Twins" at the AMC Theater in Century City. (Scott Downie, Celebrity Photo)

Chapter 17

Clint Eastwood

In real life, Clint Eastwood is an ordinary guy. Sure he's one of the world's wealthiest and most popular movie stars, but he thinks Hollywood is a strange place. Especially for raising kids. So early in his career, he packed up his young family and moved to the Northern California coastal town of Carmel where they've lived ever since.

Clint's a shade tree mechanic who works on his own cars. And, although he's owned a Ferrari and other luxury liners, he's often left them in the garage and driven his old tan Chevy pick-up truck to town on errands.

He came from a working class family, never had anything handed to him when he was younger and has had to work hard his whole life. Now at the end of a day, he enjoys having a few cold beers with the boys at the local tavern. And, like millions of other ordinary guys, Clint's divorced and has had to satisfy himself with exercising visitation rights with his two children.

Clinton Eastwood, Jr., was born May 30, 1930 in San Francisco. The depression was raging and his dad, a laborer, couldn't hold a job. Little Clint actually attended eight different grade schools on the West Coast while his family drifted and looked for work. For a time, his parents sent him to live with his grandmother on her chicken farm.

After high school, Clint worked as a lumberjack in Oregon, a steel roustabout in Texas and a gas station attendant. He joined the Army during the Korean War and taught survival training and swimming to new recruits.

The GI bill turned out to be his ticket to Hollywood-- he used it to move to Los Angeles and attend college there. He met and married attractive Maggie Johnson in 1953 and she worked as a model to help out financially while Clint tried to break into show business.

That same year, Universal Studios put him on the payroll at $75 a week and enrolled him in their acting classes. In his free time, Clint wandered around movie sets trying to learn everything he could about the business. Although the studio did give him a small part as a lab assistant in *Revenge of the Creature*, they fired him a short time later after telling him he simply didn't have what it took to be a movie star. Clint then got a job digging swimming pools around town. His big break came in 1958, when a producer for the new CBS-TV western *Rawhide* was struck by his rugged face while Clint was eating at an L.A. cafeteria. Eastwood, at 27, was quickly offered the role of cattle boss Rowdy Yates in the show; and for the next seven years, he kicked up trail dust driving cattle across the Western plains.

While weekly series television is an exhausting grind, *Rawhide* turned out to be Clint's launching pad to movie superstardom. When CBS would discontinue filming the show for a few months at the end of each TV season, Clint headed straight for Italy where his movie acting was in high demand. During those years, he starred as a grim, sour-tempered gunslinger with few words and no name in *Fistful of Dollars, For A Few Dollars More* and *The Good, The Bad and The Ugly*.

Enormously popular at the box office, those spaghetti westerns established Clint as a major film star and when the last steer was finally branded on *Rawhide* in 1966, he devoted all of his time to the movies. Since then, he's starred in 40 major films and has also directed 12 of them at the same time. Typically playing unsmiling tough guys and quiet, pensive loners, his hits have included *High Plains Drifter, Pale Rider, The Outlaw Josey Wales, Escape From Alcatraz, Firefox* and *Every Which Way But Loose*. One of his most memorable characters is Dirty Harry Callahan, an ice-veined San Francisco cop who thinks the courts, the law and establishment police procedures are giving criminals a break at the expense of innocent victims. Dirty Harry goes about evening the score by shoving his cannon-like magnum revolver in bad guys' faces, squinting his cold steel eyes and delivering through clenched teeth such lines as, "Go ahead, make my day."

He became the world's most popular film actor--no star in the history of motion pictures had ever drawn more people to the theatre. But as he was climbing to the top of his profession on the rocks of Alcatraz and the backs of cranky horses, rumors began circulating in Hollywood that his 25-year marriage to Maggie was foundering. Too, the word was out that Clint's relationship with comely blonde co-star Sondra Locke was turning romantic.

The question of whether his marriage was crumbling was put to Clint by Esquire interviewers after he and Locke filmed *Gauntlet.* He was quoted as bluntly replying that Maggie "has total freedom--and I want it, too. There's no ownership in this marriage. No one can own me. Mag knows this."

In December, 1979, Clint and Maggie separated after 26 years of marriage and he moved out of the house. Although neither of them filed for divorce at the time, Clint was free to openly date the 33-year-old Locke. From that point on, he and Sondra did nothing to hide their relationship and were seen together constantly.

Clint was like a lovestruck schoolboy as they cavorted. But the National Enquirer so infuriated him with a story in 1982 reporting that he was considering leaving Locke for Tanya Tucker that he hit them with a stinging $20 million lawsuit. The article, under the headline "Clint Eastwood in Love Triangle," reported that he and Locke quarreled one night when she tried to pressure him into marriage. Readers were told that Locke walked out on him, that Clint went straight to Aspen, Colorado, without her, and that he met Tanya Tucker there and was swept off his feet by her.

Clint was livid. Wrongly reporting that Tanya meant as much to him as his cherished girlfriend Sondra were fighting words to Dirty Harry. Protesting that the Enquirer story was all lies, Clint sued the tabloid for invasion of privacy and asked the court for money damages to compensate him for the mental anguish the story caused him.

His lawsuit charged that the Enquirer "published the offending article maliciously, willfully and wrongfully, with the intent to injure and disgrace Eastwood." And, he complained they did so knowing the story was false or being so reckless in their reporting that they disregarded the truth of what really happened in Aspen.

The Enquirer fought Clint tooth and nail in the courts, defending its story with the argument that disgruntled celebrities are prevented from ever suing over news reports published about them because once they become so famous, they lose their right to privacy. At that point, it contended, the public acquires a right to know about their lives.

The trial judge agreed and tossed out Clint's suit. But the California Court of Appeals, in a December 1983 ruling, rejected the tabloid's defense and overruled the trial judge. The higher court held that the press does not enjoy a privilege to report false news accounts about celebrities and that if Clint could prove the Enquirer knew the story was false or was reckless with the facts, he could win.

The appellate justices then sent the case back to the trial court to give Clint another day in court. No further court proceedings have been reported.

By 1984, it was clear to Maggie and Clint that there was no point in holding out any more hope for their marriage, and on May 16th of that year Maggie filed a Petition for Dissolution of Marriage in the Monterey County Courthouse.

Clint directed his lawyers to settle the case out of court and on November 13 they reported to Judge Richard M. Silver that a written settlement agreement had been reached dividing the millions of dollars in property.

Clint was so adamant about keeping all the details secret, he didn't even allow the Judge to review it or approve it. As long as Maggie was satisfied with the terms, Judge Silver didn't demand to see the agreement either; and on November 19, 1984 his Honor entered a terse two paragraph decree dissolving the marriage.

A review of the courthouse records reveals that legal custody of Kyle and Alison, who were then 16 and 12 years old respectively, was awarded to Clint and Maggie jointly and Maggie was given sole physical custody. The kids would live with her. Clint was granted the right to visit his children and have them spend days with him at "all reasonable times."

The secret settlement Maggie received has been estimated by knowledgeable sources to be a cool $20 million dollars. She also got the couple's awesome round red-wood home built on a cliff overlooking the Pacific Ocean near the Pebble Beach golf course. Surrounded by twelve acres of natural wilderness where deer wander among the native cypress trees, the house is perched atop the rocky coast with one solid glass wall to capture the stunning view of the ocean lapping around it.

Clint moved into a smaller stone and redwood house a few miles away and a block from the beach. A six-foot-high fence around it helps maintain his privacy. He also bought a home in Los Angeles to use when he's there on business. He already had a ranch in Northern California which he used as a retreat.

A caring and sensitive father who is deeply attached to his kids, Clint has exercised his visitation rights frequently over the years. He has picked the kids up at Maggie's and taken Kyle to the movies and Alison to riding school. They've played PacMan and other video arcade games together. When he takes them out of Carmel, they'll usually either go to his ranch for a weekend of fun or join him on location for the filming of a new movie.

In the winters, he and Sondra Locke and the children go skiing together. But even when you're Clint Eastwood, not every visitation goes smoothly. Once, both kids got the flu and were throwing up in his trailer on the set as he was racing to get their clothes packed and drive them home to their mother. He told co-workers that bringing two sick kids home after visitation meant Maggie would give him hell when he got there.

Clint's way of coping with the stress of being a single father whose ex-wife has custody of the kids? He does transcendental meditation without fail twice a day. Meditating keeps him mellow and helps him eliminate tension and pressure in his life. He was quoted by a neighbor in Carmel as saying, "I don't get uptight or worried because worrying doesn't do any good."

He is openly and enthusiastically affectionate toward his children, cuddling them and giving them bear hugs whenever they're together. The toughest guy in the movies is a real softie when it comes to his kids.

Although Clint directed Alison in a supporting part in *Tightrope* as the cop's 12-year-old daughter, Kyle is the one who is enthusiastically following in Dad's Chinese Theatre footprints. Co-starring with Clint in *Honkeytonk Man* at 14, Kyle has stayed close to his dad and tried to learn all he could from him about the movie business. In 1986, he entered the University of Southern California as a cinema major and began quietly preparing himself to carry on the family name in the industry.

But, stormclouds were forming over Carmel that year. The powerful Mayor and city council were pushing the townspeople around and butting into their lives. Local ordinances were enacted to make it illegal to wear high heels in town or to play frisbee in the park. No franchise fast food restaurants were allowed in town and no sandwiches could be sold by anybody within the city limits. Citizens were warned not to eat any food on the streets as they walked along on their way to work, school or shopping. The council refused to allow an ice cream parlor in town because it would cause litter in the streets. And, it denied Clint a permit to build a small two-story office building on a lot he owned next to his Hog's Breath Inn tavern.

Over a few cool ones at the Hog's Breath and Bud's Pub nearby, the townspeople banded together to fight back and kick the bullies out of office. Clint himself was mad enough that he ran for Mayor and led the uprising. Others got up the courage to run for council seats against the incumbents. Clint campaigned door-to-door down every street in that town of 5,000 population, telling voters that the local government was exercising too much control over their lives. He called the Mayor and council "fuddy-duddies" who were stifling the town with too many rules and regulations. He touched a nerve with voters when honestly explaining he was angry because he felt it just wasn't the American way for government to push people around like that.

In the April, 1986 local election, Clint unseated the incumbent Mayor by a landslide margin of three-to-one atop a record-breaking turnout of voters who rallied to his cause. Sitting council members who Clint had targeted were also overwhelmingly voted out of office. Mayor Dirty Harry and the townspeople wasted no time in retaking control of their town and, as soon as they assumed office, changes were made. They repealed the no-ice cream cone law, built a new library annex, increased parking spaces downtown and turned city government around to where now it works for the townspeople--not against them.

But while Clint's foray into politics was consistent with the populist, anti-establishment political philosophies of many of the characters he's played, it has been somewhat of a departure from the way he has so assiduously lived his private life. He is still a loner, really, who keeps most of his thoughts to himself and who is a man of few words even while drinking with the boys. He hardly ever talks about his personal life except to express a father's pride in something one of his children has done.

He exercises by himself every day, jogging on the beach for a mile or more and then working out in the gym in his home for two hours to classical music. He likes to play golf or tennis in the afternoons for fun. In great shape, he tries to eat healthy foods like avocados stuffed with tuna, but will often enjoy eating a greasy hot dog smothered with everything.

Is he ever going to make it official with Sondra Locke? "I've had one marriage that didn't work and I don't know if I'd want to do that again," he told <u>People</u> interviewers bluntly.

Well, what advice do you have for other ordinary guys trying to survive tough times? Clint would say know yourself, shut out all self-doubt and gut your way through.

And he's proved it.

Former Congresswoman, Cabinet Secretary and Ambassador Margaret Heckler. (Photo: American Embassy, Dublin, Ireland)

Chapter 18

Margaret Heckler

Boston financier John Heckler filed divorce papers against his wife in 1983 charging that she had cut him off in 1963 and refused to engage in any marital cohabitation since then. He claimed his wife Margaret, the former eight-term Republican Congresswoman from Massachusetts and then Secretary of Health and Human Services in President Reagan's Cabinet, lost all interest in sex when she began her political career. Yes, she had denied him his own human services. And, while it took him 20 years to complain about it, he was hopping mad now.

She had become a workaholic, climbing the political ladder and living life in Washington's fast lane. There was apparently no stopping for sex on the way to the top.

When Fairfax County Deputy Sheriff S. H. Lewis served those papers on Secretary Heckler in her Arlington, Virginia, condominium at 10:15 a.m. on December 10, 1983, official Washington braced itself. The dirty laundry of a member of Ronald Reagan's inner circle was about to be hung from the Capitol flagpole.

In contrast to the British, who seem to stir up at least one juicy sex scandal in each Prime Minister's term in office, this would be a reverse sex scandal. That is, the scandal was that there was no sex. Some cynics would laugh that it is as good as the Reagan administration could do for a sex scandal, and that it was little wonder there are so many more Democrats than Republicans in Massachusetts.

But there was guano in the Heckler case and it was ready to hit the fan. It was bound to come out that John had covert relationships with other women for years. Margaret reportedly allowed him that infidelity in order to keep their marriage together and present a picture of family bliss to the voters every two years. Next, as her campaign manager and confidante, John had also witnessed twenty years of behind-the-scenes Washington wheeling and dealing. Would he sing like a canary? And, there were all his bawdy charges about Margaret the marital iceberg ready to be splattered across the pages of the nation's newspapers.

The Secretary decided to act. She filed a motion to dismiss John's complaint on the grounds that they were both technically residents of Massachusetts and, therefore, Virginia courts did not have jurisdiction to hear the case. At the same time, she asked the Judge to seal the file from the press, withhold all pleadings and documents from the public and conduct all proceedings in chambers so that no one else could learn anything about the case or hear any more of John's sordid allegations. She even sought an order prohibiting John and his attorneys from talking about the case to reporters.

Then, fearing that John's tantalizing disclosures would rock the White House, she went directly to President Reagan and told him a bitter divorce was brewing. She explained to him that she feared the press would have a field day, and she didn't want to cause him any political embarrassment. The President was understanding and supportive. Margaret told the Associated Press after their meeting that Reagan "said he had been through a divorce himself and he knew how painful it was." He comforted her by observing that she had raised three wonderful children and was a very good mother to them. She told UPI reporters on the scene that Reagan "reassured me this would in no way affect me. I will be judged on my professional record and my performance." With the President's backing, she was ready to stand up to John.

To put the Heckler case into wider context, it is sadly representative of many Congressional marriages. The only difference is that, here, it was the husband who was the helpmate and loyal supporter. In the end, John complained that he had dedicated thirty years of his life to promoting Margaret's political ambitions, actually managing many of her winning Congressional campaigns and making thousands of public appearances for her.

She spent the weeks in Washington; he stayed home in Boston running the campaigns and building his investment banking business. They would see each other only on weekends when campaigning together.

As Margaret moved up in seniority and national stature, her career demands increased astronomically. There was even less time to spend with John, and he found himself in the lowly position of having to compete for her time and attention.

And as she was becoming intoxicated by the power of national office and as politics became her total life, the marital bed went cold. People magazine quoted a friend as saying, "she is asexual--her mind was always on politics." John admitted to UPI that "the longer we were married, the more obvious" it became that she was married "to the public . . . and her career came first."

It is interesting to note, however, that having a wife in Congress didn't hurt John's investment business at all. John always made the point in his company brochures that his wife was a Congresswoman and he took advantage of the Washington financial contacts which were opened to him. Citing the use of Margaret's name in his business, one former campaign aide commented to UPI reporters, "He got what he wanted out of the marriage."

In fact, it was at John's urging that Margaret entered the Boston College Law School just one month after their 1953 marriage in New York's St. Patrick's Cathedral. So, she was never a traditional homemaker; she was a career woman from the beginning, and she was determined to be a lawyer. Women rarely went into law in the early 1950s and she was the only female in her class. She worked circles around her male counterparts and was named editor of the law review and winner of the moot court competition-- the two principal indicators of being the best in the class. She graduated in 1956 only to encounter reluctance on the part of Boston's prestigious, conservative law firms to hire a woman lawyer. Her response was typical Heckler feistiness--she set up her own law office with several of her classmates and competed head on with the established firms.

In her spare time, she worked as a volunteer in local Republican campaigns. In 1962, she ran for Governor's council and John organized her dark horse campaign. Her slogan was "You need a Heckler on the Governor's Council." She won and was re-elected in 1964. By 1966, this determined and ambitious lady was ready for bigger stakes and she jolted the Boston Republican establishment by challenging veteran Congressman Joseph W. Martin in the primary. Martin, who had served 21 years in the House of Representatives and a term as Speaker, was considered a shoo-in and the party big wigs paid little attention to Margaret.

This, too, was a time when women candidates for Congress were few and far between. Was the venerable Congressman going to worry about some lady? No way. But John ran her campaign and women rallied to her side. She upset Martin in the primary, went on to win the general election, and was re-elected every two years for 16 straight years. She was one of only two Republican national office holders from the liberal Democratic bastion of Massachusetts.

From those lonely years in law school when she was the only woman to her formidable campaign later to win a seat in Congress and then hold onto it, Margaret flashed real courage when the going got tough. The only child of Irish Catholic immigrants to America, she had it in her blood. She was strong and tenacious.

In her years in the Congress, she earned a reputation as a vigorous proponent of women's and consumers' rights and enthusiastically supported the Equal Rights Amendment. Yet, she was a bundle of contradictions as a Congresswoman--a feminist from one of the most liberal states who was at the same time an ardent supporter of Ronald Reagan. She had the President's ear. Reagan liked her non-confrontational, non-belligerent approach in presenting feminist views. In fact, Margaret is credited with Sandra Day O'Connor's appointment to the Supreme Court as a result of her firm and direct request to Reagan to name a woman if he got the opportunity. <u>Boston</u> magazine once reported that Reagan "just melts when he's around her."

Good thing for her, as it turned out. After her Congressional district was gerrymandered, she was defeated in her 1982 bid for re-election. She sought appointment to a top job in the Reagan administration and the President gave her a real plum--a Cabinet post. She was named the Secretary of Health and Human Services with the responsibility for 145,000 employees and an annual budget of $276 billion.

On March 4, 1983, the Senate swiftly confirmed her appointment and she became one of the Cabinet's thirteen members. Immediately, a presidential security force began protecting her. Agents picked her up each morning at her Arlington condominium in a Lincoln limousine and took her to the HHS offices in downtown Washington. Her bodyguards knew her daily schedule hours in advance and inspected every place she would later appear, including restaurants where she planned to have dinner.

Former aides confirm she was at her HHS office twenty hours a day and was a workaholic who drove herself and her staff beyond all reasonable limits. Bright, with a steel-trap mind, she was intolerant of subordinates' blunders and was typically short with everyone. She was described as a 5'2", 110 pound jumble of nervous energy, who was restless and intense. No one could remember seeing her relaxed while in office or her ever showing any sense of humor.

As the highest ranking woman in the Reagan administration, Margaret addressed the 1984 Republican National Convention in Dallas along with other top GOP women officeholders to counter Walter Mondale's selection of Geraldine Ferraro as his running mate.

And John was always the man behind the woman. What happened to this marriage was that he grew tired of that role. After thirty years as Mr. Mom, he wanted out. He threatened to "tell all" if Margaret gave him any trouble.

He should've known that his wife was nothing if not a fighter. She, in fact, refused to roll over and the bout was on. Her attorney filed a demand for all photographs, movies or tapes in John's possession that he intended to use as evidence of her refusal to cohabitant with him. Then, they pressed their argument with the judge in Virginia that the case should properly be heard in Massachusetts. John tried to keep it in Virginia because he didn't want the case to be heard in a courtroom back in Margaret's old Congressional district. But the judge agreed with Margaret and the scene of the battle shifted to the Boston suburb of Dedham.

Since their three children were all grown, child custody wasn't an issue. What they were battling about was money and how to divide up their marital property. They owned a $300,000 Arlington condo overlooking the Potomac and a classy 19th century home in genteel Wellesley, Massachusetts. The major asset, though, was John's highly successful investment business which reported $9 million in sales the year before.

John felt Margaret was trying to gouge him and protested to UPI that his wife was worth $500,000 more than him but she was still demanding a $1.9 million dollar divorce settlement "including a million dollars I don't have." Sticking in his craw also was the fact that to help her in her last Congressional campaign, he personally borrowed $92,000 and had to repay all of it himself. He complained that she was a millionairess in her own right, having recently inherited big money from her parents. On top of that, he calculated that she was earning over $100,000 a year from her Cabinet salary and investments.

John was willing to divide all their joint assets 50-50, but Margaret had her sights set on his business and she wanted a chunk of it for thirty years time in. They fought tooth and nail over that business and simply could not reach any out-of-court agreement. The stage was set for the divorce trial of the century involving a Cabinet member.

On January 9, 1985, Massachusetts Probate Judge Edmund V. Keville strode to the bench and gaveled the trial of Heckler vs. Heckler to order. Sitting at the counsel table with her lawyer, Margaret nervously clenched and unclenched her fists while Edward Lev, John's lawyer, delivered a stinging opening statement. He admitted John had committed adultery during the marriage, but that Margaret had forced her husband into it by refusing to engage in marital relations with him. Lev blasted Margaret for condemning John "to a life of either celibacy or adultery," and told the Judge that Margaret had condoned John's adultery for her own political purposes, fearing a divorce would have hurt her in the eyes of the voters. Lev argued Margaret had abandoned the marriage for politics years before. "Her political ambitions were all-consuming," he explained.

Margaret's attorney, Jeffrey Rosenfield, took a different tack in his opening statement, choosing the high road. Refusing to personally attack John, Rosenfield told Judge Keville that "Margaret Heckler's main concern is to protect the dignity of the marriage, the children and the family."

But the trial quickly hunkered down to a dry and tedious exercise in estimating the value of John's business. Lawyers for both sides slogged through countless financial records and introduced reams of business reports. John's attorneys claimed the business was worth $800,000; Margaret's countered that it was worth four times that much and that John was lowballing it just to keep Margaret's share as small as possible.

Two days into the trial, John took a seat in the back of the wood-paneled courtroom as the five attorneys continued their haggling over finances. Samuel Adams, one of Margaret's four lawyers, sought to prohibit John from taking the witness stand and spilling his guts to all the reporters stacked up in the gallery. He told the Judge that since John took the Fifth Amendment during his pre-trial deposition and refused to answer the question whether he had committed adultery on the grounds he might incriminate himself, he should be barred from testifying about anything else at the trial. (There was a six-year statute of limitations for prosecution of adultery, and if John had admitted it he could have been charged.) The Judge reserved ruling on the request until later in the trial.

Margaret would testify first, anyway. But the trial dragged on as each side called expert witnesses to the stand with differing assessments of the value of the business. On January 17, Judge Keville adjourned the trial for a three-day weekend so that Margaret could participate in President Reagan's second inauguration in Washington. She was expected to testify right after the inaugural ceremonies.

When the trial resumed, John's attorneys turned the tables on Margaret. They started calling witnesses to value the worth of her Congressional and Cabinet pension. Margaret had said all along it was worth $158,000. Claude Poulin, an actuary from Washington, testified that in reality it had a $425,000 cash value. John claimed he was entitled to a share of it because he was the one who managed all her campaigns that kept her in office long enough to even earn a pension.

By February 11, the attorneys were still haggling over the value of the marital assets and neither John nor Margaret had yet taken the witness stand. For four weeks, that courtroom sounded like the newsrooms at Barron's or The Wall Street Journal. There was electricity in the air, though, because both sides had run out of expert economists and appraisers. Margaret was up next and it was a sure bet that, on cross-examination, John's lawyer would be asking her more than just questions about the weather. From his vituperative opening salvo, reporters knew he would go straight for Margaret's jugular. The trial would quickly shift from money to sex and politics. The tension mounted as the expert witnesses shoveled away their boxes of papers and reports. It was showtime.

At that very moment, Judge Keville decided to intervene. He called Margaret and John into his chambers and spoke with them for 75 minutes. The Judge encouraged them to settle their differences, divide up the assets and avoid further courtroom agony. He provided them some general guidelines for valuing their property and dividing it up in a manner fair to both. After meeting with the Judge, Margaret told reporters that she'd make every effort to settle and that she was hopeful it could be done. She characterized the Judge as very sensitive and principled. Judge

Keville recessed the trial for the next two days while the attorneys worked around the clock to hammer out a financial settlement.

On February 13, it was over. Margaret and John agreed to the terms contained in a 40-page settlement agreement which divided their assets. The Judge reviewed and approved it and sealed it from ever being seen by the press or the public. However, it was later revealed that Margaret would keep the Arlington condo and John would sell the Wellesley home.

Under Massachusetts law, the divorce would become final nine months later.

Margaret had been spared testifying about all of John's allegations and she was noticeably relieved. She admitted that since the first divorce papers were served, it had been a very painful time for her.

Before they left the courthouse, Margaret and John shook hands one last time and wished each other well. They expressed the hope that some day they could be friendly again. Margaret acknowledged to the press that "we're very happy it's over, particularly for the children."

Eight months later, Margaret was removed from the Cabinet and named U.S. Ambassador to Ireland. Some Washington insiders cited her inefficient management of the monstrous HHS as the reason, but others insisted her extremely public and brutal divorce tarnished her image among the White House guard.

She served energetically and capably as Ambassador until resigning in early 1989, amid speculation she would return to Massachusetts and run for Governor when Michael Dukakis' term expires in 1990. As a Republican, if she does campaign for Governor in that heavily Democratic state, it will be trench warfare.

But Margaret Heckler knows how to weather both political and personal adversity--by being tough, holding her head high and looking to the future. It worked in her divorce.

Her philosophy in dealing with divorce was New England stoic and practical. She told UPI reporters it was "time to put the past behind [. . . me and] go on with the challenges and excitements of this life." As she explained to the Washington Post: "A marriage that produced such beautiful children is nothing to be sorry for."

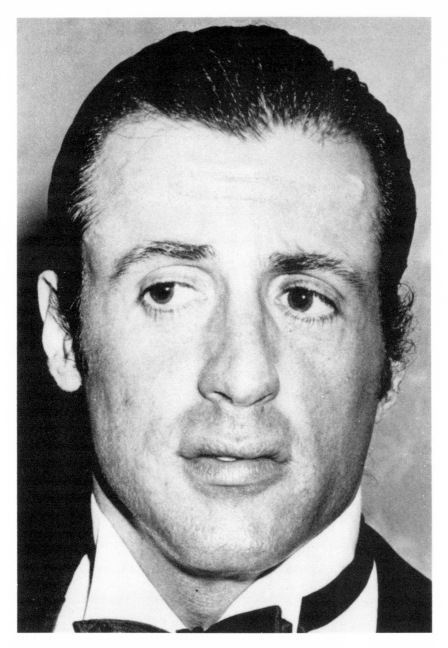

Sylvester Stallone at the 1988 White House Correspondents' Annual Dinner at the Washington Hilton Hotel. (Victor Malafronte, Celebrity Photo)

Chapter 19

Sylvester Stallone

Sylvester Stallone's life from rags to Rambo is a story-book American dream--with an Italian Stallion twist. For him, in fact, it's been an American wet dream. And, his years at stud have not only cost him tens of millions of dollars in court for several affairs and two divorces, but branded him an alleycat by some in Hollywood.

Ironically, Stallone never would have made it out of the Lincoln Tunnel without the help of his first wife, Sasha. In 1969, he was starving as a 22-year-old writer and actor, unable to find work in New York City. It got so bad that once, just to eat, he stripped naked for $200 and rutted with a roomful of ten other horny exhibitionists in a cheap porno flick, starring as Studs in *Party at Kitty and Stud's*. Later, he landed odd jobs to keep him going, including one at Central Park Zoo for $1.12 an hour cleaning out the lion cages each day. Not only was shoveling out after the lions a dirty job, Sly suffered the indignity of being urinated on by the territorial beasts when he'd slink into their cages. Other resume builders from his years struggling in New York were wrapping smelly fish in a market and ushering in a movie theatre.

He met young Sasha Czack in 1970 and love blossomed. Soon, they were living together and Sasha was working three jobs from 8:00 a.m. to 1:00 a.m. every day to support them.

Sly was spending his time writing movie scripts, which Sasha would type for him at night. He was developing a skill for quick script writing and was amazingly productive, in terms of quantity if not yet quality. He even wrote one movie which chronicled the life of a rock musician whose appetite for bananas ruined his career. (It's true!) There were many times during the lean years when it seemed Sly was never going to make it as a writer, as the ghosts of the straight D's he got in high school and his college freshman class rank of 97th out of 97 clanked their chains. This was not exactly Kurt Vonnegut in his study. But Sasha believed in him and stood by him.

In 1974, they got a break. A producer liked a script Sly had written for a horror film and sent him cash for it. It was just a few hundred dollars, but to Sly and Sasha, it was all the proof they needed that Vonnegut just got some new competition. Invigorated and feeling prosperous, they bought a 10-year-old beater of a car for $40, turned it to the West and headed for Hollywood to claim their place in the sun. Renting a shabby apartment near Sunset Strip in downtown L.A. and affirming their faith in the future by getting married on December 28, 1974 after living together for five years, they positioned themselves for a rendezvous with destiny.

Sasha was several months pregnant and they were down to $106 in the bank when Sly took a chunk of their cash and bought himself a ticket to the Ali-Wepner championship boxing match in early 1975. Wepner, the unknown underdog who was obviously no match for Mohammud Ali in size or skill, stunned the crowd by going the distance against the champ. The more rounds the little scrapper survived against Ali's crushing firepower, the more wildly the spectators roared for him; and by the end of the match, most fans were on their feet cheering for him. Stallone was stirred by the electricity around him in that auditorium. Inspired, he ran home and, over the next four days, feverishly dictated to Sasha the script for a film based on what he'd seen. He called it *Rocky.*

Rocky Balboa, the Italian Stallion, was a losing small-time boxer who was going nowhere with his drab life. When given the chance to be sacrificed to heavyweight champion Apollo Creed, Balboa reached down within himself and ignited a spark that propelled him through several months of grueling training to upset Creed in a sensational match. Along the way, he won the hearts of everyone who'd ever been an underdog in life.

When he read it over, Sly knew he had written a spectacular movie. But in a flash of guts most broke writers could never have shown, he refused to sell it to any film studio unless they'd let him star as Rocky. He turned down offers of hundreds of thousands of dollars from studios that wanted the script but insisted on letting an established star like Burt Reynolds, Paul Newman or Robert Redford take the lead. Sly stuck to his guns, however, and finally signed a deal with United Artists whereby he'd star as Rocky, all right, but would only be paid peanuts for his acting. After all, he was an unknown. The studio did agree to pay him a percentage of the profits if the movie made anything.

For the next five months, the flabby Sly devoted his life to getting in shape to portray a professional boxer. The task before him was to remake himself into a new person physically, and he did it one drop of sweat at a time. He worked from first light to lights out every day - running five miles, living at the gym and pounding the stuffing out of the medicine ball. He sparred with real boxers, pulverized the punching bag, lifted heavy weights and gulped down 130 vitamin pills each day. Five painful months later, he had the body of a pro boxer and he played Rocky Balboa to a T.

A T-bill that is, because the film was a colossal hit and one of the most popular movies ever made. It not only grossed $250 million at box offices across the country, it touched people's hearts and 29-year-old Sylvester Stallone became the newest American folk hero. *Rocky* won the Academy Award as Best Picture of 1976 and for Sly, who had earned $1,400 in income the entire previous year, it made him a millionaire. In fact, his first *Rocky* paycheck for his percentage of the profits was for a cool million in cash and was delivered to him in an armored truck.

But sudden success and wealth changed Stallone into a heel. One of the first things he did was to have a passionate and very public affair with shapely young actress Joyce Ingalls, apparently figuring that was a wild oats perk to which big movie stars were entitled. Sasha, whom he left behind with their 22-month-old baby while he was out shaking his manhood, disagreed. She thought he was an ungrateful cad for walking out on her when he got to the top; and, on March 17, 1978 she filed a petition for divorce in the Los Angeles Superior Court.

Describing Sly's recent strange behavior, she stated in court documents that in February he "paid for a vacation for himself and a girlfriend, one Joyce Ingalls, to New York and Hawaii; using our community property funds." And, she feared the lovestruck Sly "will continue to give away our ... funds to Ms. Ingalls." Intent on preventing Sly from blowing all his Rocky money on his sex kitten at the expense of his wife and child, Judge Norman Pittluck entered a temporary restraining order against Sly on March 17 preventing him from spending funds acquired before the separation on his paramour.

Three months later, Sly returned home to Sasha, pleading for forgiveness and admitting he'd been a fool. He told her he was sorry and she took him back on the spot. On May 8, 1978 they confirmed for the Court that they had reconciled and Judge Pittluck dismissed Sasha's petition.

At home, things returned to the way they were before stardom set in. In that atmosphere of warmth and sensitivity for each other, Sly penned *Rocky II*--an emotional, tender masterpiece which focused primarily on Rocky and Adrian's love story, their family life and Rocky as a devoted father.

Sasha gave birth to a second child, Sergio, on May 17, 1979 and all appearances were that their little family was charting new dimensions in bliss.

But in June of that year, *Rocky II* opened in theatres nationwide and quickly became that year's hottest movie. Sly was jettisoned to a plateau of super stardom few have ever achieved and the tidal wave from his newest success capsized his cozy marriage. More accurately, Captain Sly jumped ship again.

The phenomenal success of *Rocky II* thrust Sly back into the national limelight as Hollywood's top star and he just couldn't do justice to that role while lazily watering his lawn in the suburbs. Partying and snaking beckoned him; so he left Sasha and the kids on July 1, 1979--six weeks after Sergio's birth.

This time, he found the good life in the arms and legs of Susan Anton, a six-foot-tall blonde who could win any wet shorts contest in the country. A former Miss Arizona runner-up and sultry spokeswoman on several Muriel Cigars TV commercials, Anton set up housekeeping with Sly in a comfortable Malibu Beach house right on the ocean.

Anguished, Sasha returned to the Los Angeles County Courthouse and filed for divorce on July 6, 1979.

Sly and Anton romped. They flaunted their tryst, even to the point of Sly appearing with Susan in her flashy Las Vegas nightclub act for six weeks. Susan didn't even want to keep their sex life private, bragging to reporters for People that her Sly was a "wonderful lover--physically." She went ahead making wedding plans and told anyone who'd listen that she wanted to have his child.

After nine wet months, their affair ran out of gas and Sly went back to Sasha, hat in hand. Once burned, she refused to take him back and instead sent him away to repent and get a grip on his life and lust. He decided the best place to do all that, and to film his newest movie, *Victory*, at the same time was in Budapest. Then, he set sail to find the meaning of life in the Hungarian hinterlands.

And sure enough, after a few celibate weeks there, he found it and hurriedly telephoned Sasha back in the States to join him right away so he could reveal it to her. And after reportedly consulting her astrologist, she was Budapest bound--and was told by the stubbly nouveau guru when she got there that what had been messing him up was a mistaken mindset that every day in his life had to be Saturday night. She bought it and after one more call to the astrologist, she took him home where on November 12, 1980 she withdrew her divorce petition.

As had their last reconciliation, this reunion with Sasha ignited a creative spurt in Sly which saw him pen *Rocky III* and develop the character of John Rambo for *First Blood*. Both gigantic successes, *Rocky III* introduced Mr. T as Rocky's latest opponent and was such a box office smash that Stallone was elevated to posterity on the cover of Time magazine. *First Blood*, with Rambo being hunted through the wilderness of the Pacific Northwest and fighting back by personally annihilating a small town, was a blockbuster hit. Striking a nerve in millions of Americans, *Rambo* became a part of our culture and went on in *First Blood: Part II* to give the public more blood.

On the home front, the bedsprings were bouncing and Sly even had workers install a bedside computer so he could dial up a neon light show in the darkened bedroom each night with 7,000 color visual effects for stimulating the senses. Given his Italian Stallion libido, he probably didn't need more than a flashlight with a weak battery to turn him on, but the fancy strobe lights added a new dimension.

Tragedy struck in 1983 when little 3-year-old Sergio was diagnosed as autistic by his doctors. Autism, a form of mental retardation in which the victim often doesn't learn to talk and shies away from most human contact, hits families hard. Sasha and Sly's reaction was to establish the Stallone Fund for Autism to raise money to find a cure; and Sly has funneled hundreds of thousands of dollars into the foundation by donating all the proceeds from the premiers of his many movies. Sasha has devoted virtually her entire life to running the foundation and patiently working with Sergio daily to try to bring him out of his dark world.

But the marriage was doomed. As Sly's friends saw it, Sasha had become plain obsessed with her work with autistic kids and blown him off. From Sasha's perspective, people figured that after all the affairs and heavy breathing whenever a young starlet walked by, it had come to the point that she simply didn't trust him anymore.

In November, 1984 Sly moved out for the third time and Sasha quickly filed for divorce. She had been to the courthouse before, of course, but this time she stuck to her guns. And, in one of the longest divorces in Hollywood history, her attorneys tried to stick it to Sly.

At first, it appeared the divorce would be a smooth one. Within a few months, they agreed to a partial settlement which awarded custody of the children to Sasha and provided her at least $12 million. That chunk represented one half of the accumulations of the marriage, to which she was entitled by California's community property law. On top of that, she got child support and alimony.

Sly took his half and invested millions in $100,000 CDs at banks all over Southern California, formed his own closely-held corporations to invest in real estate development and bought several luxury automobiles.

On July 31, 1985 Judge Pro Tem Kenneth A. Black entered an order dissolving the marriage and approving the terms of the settlement agreement. The divorce was proved up easily, with only Sly and his attorney present in court for the hearing. At the time, it was understood between Sly and Sasha that what remained to be resolved was the division of any interest in Sly's name and goodwill to which she might be entitled for helping him make it to the top, whether she had a right to any Rambo income received after they separated and the results of an accounting of the assets of Sly's corporations.

From that July until April of 1986, the attorneys cooperated with each other in answering the remaining questions. Sly allowed Sasha's accountants, appraisers and lawyers full and unrestricted access to the books and records of all his companies and to every piece of paper and financial document in his possession.

On April 25, 1986 Sly's accountants presented Sasha with a detailed itemization of some $37 million in assets which Sly insisted were his separate property--assets which he claimed Sasha could not get her hands on. The wealth on that 29-page document consisted primarily of investments Sly had made with his half of the community property millions he and Sasha had divied up the preceding year and a few more million he'd earned from new movies *Rhinestone* (1984) and *First Blood: Part II* (1985). The list reveals what Sly got in the settlement, how he has invested the millions he has made and the kinds of things he buys for himself. For instance, he sunk $2 million in CD's, $450,000 in Treasury bills and $188,000 in gold and silver. He put $20 million into new companies he formed to build apartment buildings, homes and offices in New York, Michigan, Tennessee, Arkansas and Missouri. One of his companies bought the Holiday Inn in Gainesville, Florida.

His companies moved in style, too. One of them, Rogue Marble Corporation, was outfitted with a $72,000 1986 Mercedes Benz 1000 SEL, a $303,000 1985 Prevost LeMirage LX, a $22,000 1985 Cadillac Fleetwood and a $35,000 1986 Chevy Suburban for its garages in case the boss would stop by and want to inspect any of his investments by car. At home, Sly also had seven cars including a 1950 Ford, 1950 Mercury, 1958 Chevy, 1964 Corvette, 1985 Porsche, 1958 Ferrari and 1985 Mercedes.

Sly bought nearly $3 million worth of unimproved lots in Hawaii, 42 pieces of rare sculpture and paintings for just under $2 million and paid $64,696 for a set of steak knives.

Home for him was a $3 million Pacific Palisades mansion, a $2,400,000 Malibu beachhouse with $10,000 a month mortgage payments, a $391,000 Santa Monica condo and a 23-acre ranch in Thousand Oaks which he bought for $1,300,000.

Having accounted for every penny to his name, Sly offered Sasha some more money from his Rambo earnings to be done with it. To his shock and surprise, she and her attorneys rejected it and suddenly took a get tough posture, demanding millions more. From then on, the attorneys for both sides dug in and waged one of the most vicious divorce battles ever fought. And, they didn't confine their fighting to the issues, either. They took every opportunity to attack each other personally and accuse each other of stupidity, laziness and lying.

The first blow below the belt was struck by Sasha's attorneys, Judith Shapiro and Ira Lurvey, when Ms. Shapiro issued a notice and subpoena to Sly demanding that he present himself so she could take his deposition in July, 1986. Shapiro obviously wasn't satisfied with Sly's 29-page financial statement and wanted to give him the third degree under oath to see if she could shake a few more million out of him. Parties to lawsuits are required to submit to such grueling examinations by opposing attorneys before trial, but what infuriated Sly was that she had scheduled his deposition right in the middle of the filming of his newest movie, *Over The Top*. In it, he played a trucker and for the picture was driving all over California and Nevada. To Sly, who works hard and breaks his back on his movies, this was pure harassment. What really ignited him was that Shapiro and Sasha knew he would be working then and they went ahead and served him with those papers anyway. Their only purpose had to be to embarrass him on location and interfere with something in which he took enormous personal pride--the filming of his movie.

Madder than a hornet, Sly filed a motion for a protective order with the judge, pleading with him to intervene and not allow the deposition until after the movie was completed.

Sasha's other attorney, Ira Lurvey, shot back that Sly was doing the old Ali shuffle in the form of a "consistent pattern of delay and obfuscation." As he saw it, Sly was just trying to dodge being asked tough questions about his $37 million. Then Mr. Lurvey queried what the big deal was, anyway, in them demanding only to depose him, noting that they hadn't asked him "to step aside from ... [filming] one of his epics of violence." Obviously, Lurvey was no Rambo fan. Ms. Shapiro bellyached, "I have been informed that Stallone boasts of how long he can delay deposition discovery."

Norman Dolin, one of Sly's lawyers, couldn't take any more of it and filed papers with the judge lambasting Shapiro and Lurvey. To Shapiro, he wrote: "Your letters are always demeaning of Mr. Stallone, contain veiled threats, which apparently you see as being some type of intimidation, and are abusive and negative." And as for Mr. Lurvey, Dolin told the judge that Lurvey's arguments were "his typical sermon from the mount, which contains so many of his irrelevancies," and that Lurvey's comments about the deposition imbroglio contained "misleading statements, untruths and inaccuracies."

Judge Black had heard enough and, in a hearing on July 29, 1986 ruled that Sasha's lawyers could not take Sly's deposition until he finished shooting the movie. Soon, the fighting cooled down.

Since the summer of 1986, Sly and Sasha have been getting along better than ever and it was reported in the press that Sly even turned to her for comfort and advice when his marriage to Brigitte Nielsen came apart. To give him a break, Sasha called off the dogs and her attorneys never again pressed him to submit to a painful deposition.

Sly had left Sasha in November, 1984; and as happened the other two times he walked out on her, he was soon sleeping with a young, long-legged blonde actress. This time, he would really get burned. Within days of separating from Sasha, Sly took a break from filming *Rocky IV* and checked into a suite at New York City's fashionable Essex House. Brigitte Nielsen, a 21-year old Danish model who had a school girl's crush on him, desperately wanted to meet him and delivered a nearly-nude photo of herself to his room. The daring, promiscuous picture showed all of the 6' model, dressed only in a mini-bikini. She was a palomino--tall, lean, built, curvaceous and with long strong legs going all the way up to her ears. Sly, predictably thinking with his pants again, absolutely could not resist and within hours they were having dinner and drinks.

For Sly, it was love at first bite. For Gitte, as she preferred to be called, who had so cunningly stalked him, it was antlers on the den wall. She was so calculating and he was so naive. They immediately started dating, he gave her the part of Drago's steroid pushing Russian wife in *Rocky IV* and within two months they were living together back in Los Angeles.

But there were things about Gitte that just didn't seem to jive and would have made a more thoughtful man cautious about the relationship. For instance, she had already shown she was capable of walking on anybody to get to the top of her chosen career. In March, 1984 she married rock musician Kasper Winding in Copenhagen, had a son by him a couple of months later, and left them both when the baby was six months old to seek stardom in the United States. Too, she was 17 years younger than Sly and five inches taller. She used skin pix of herself as calling cards and she was still very much married.

Even Stallone's outspoken mother, Jackie, was quoted by Star magazine as protesting, "I don't like the broad because I know perfectly well she just wants his money." Mom figured that Sly was "soft in the head" when it came to young blonde beauties with long legs, and that he'd be better off with a thinking girl like Diane Sawyer. But Sly was blind to what everyone else was seeing and, just before Gitte's 22nd birthday in December, 1985 they were married.

The $25,000 fur-trimmed wedding gown that she demanded should have portended the odyssey which was to follow but wedding guests John Travolta, Bruce Jenner, Victoria Principal, Donna Summer and Morgan Fairchild were there to celebrate and not to question Sly's judgment.

What happened next, in the 17 months that their ill-fated marriage held together, would make any Rambo fan cringe in shame. Gitte reportedly often aggressively wore the pants in the family, pulled Sly around in public in Hollywood and New York, manipulated him and made a run on his bank accounts. For 17 months, it could be said she used him and abused him; and, in the end, Sly couldn't take any more and sued for divorce.

The story of their brief, stormy marriage is one of stage lights, shopping sprees and shower sex. The big victim was his checkbook.

A few days before they were married, Sly had insisted that the Great Dane sign a prenuptial agreement which would deny her the right to ever claim 50% of the earnings he made during their marriage if they divorced. Perfectly legal and enforceable, that contract seemed prudent to Stallone's attorneys at the time because, after all, he was still battling Sasha over the financial payoff she'd get from his first marriage. This would be a little insurance, but in return for relinquishing her community property rights, Gitte was given several perks. First among them, as the tabloids tattled, was a rich allowance of $1,000 a day spending money. This was pocket change for her--"mad money;" and in the first four months of the marriage she reportedly blew a whole year's worth and came running to Sly for a refill.

When it came to shopping, she was a Tammy Faye Bakker and an Imelda Marcos wrapped into one. During one wild spending binge, for instance, she bought 30 pairs of shoes with price tags up to $600 a pair. She'd buy $22,000 dresses and $500 skirts. The generous kind, she gave a new jeep to her secretary, which she charged to Sly.

Often, she'd drag Sly along shopping and he looked dazed as he shuffled behind her. One New York City shop owner reported that Gitte brought Sly into his wig shop and milked $3,000 out of him for a storeful of outdated wigs by slobbering him with flattery and manipulating him with lines like she only wanted the wigs so she'd look good for him. The merchant remembers Sly looked like he was in a trance as he kept throwing out more money.

While admitting that they argued a little bit at home, Brigitte revealed that usually at night she and Rambo would horse around the house or jump in the shower together. She preened to Cosmo that "we are extreme lovers."

Sly reportedly lavished her with three-fourths of a million dollars in gifts during the marriage, including a $150,000 sports car. She was sometimes hard to please, as he found out when she complained that the teeth of the new poodle puppy he'd just given her were crooked. Sly, of course, plunked down $1,000 to have a doggy orthodontist put braces on the little thing, and Gitte was happy again. He seemed mesmerized by her physique, though, and even had a dining room table made for $20,000 with her face etched on the top.

And Brigitte was getting what she really wanted out of Sly--a movie career for herself. He gave her a plum part in *Rocky IV*, paid her a quarter of a million dollars to co-star with him in the police thriller *Cobra* and helped get her the female lead in *Beverly Hills Cop II*.

But it was during the filming of *Cop II* that Sly apparently gradually woke up to the reality that he had been used and that Gitte was much more interested in her own separate career than in him. He finally got the picture.

An explosion of stories suddenly appeared in the tabloids featuring interviews with some of Sly's friends who all confirmed he was fed up with being used by Gitte. They revealed that he was complaining to them that her favorite song was the chimes of a cash register, that the more tens of thousands he gave her the faster she spent it and that marrying her was the biggest mistake he'd ever made in his life.

On May 12, 1987, Sly told Brigitte to start packing. He then filed for divorce.

Because of the prenuptial agreement she signed just before the marriage, Gitte reportedly got more than a million in separation cash and bonuses, along with all the gifts he ladled on her and everything she bought on her legendary shopping sprees during the marriage. More important, the marriage to Sly had made her a rich, famous movie star very quickly.

But celebrating her shrewdness was cut short two months later when a London newspaper reported she was entwined in a lesbian relationship with her young personal secretary with whom she frequently traveled. The secretary vehemently denied it and Sly broke his silence to lash out at the report, saying "I am totally outraged by the fictitious allegations." Calling the story "filthy and false," he protested that Gitte "is a totally feminine woman." He must've enjoyed seeing her knocked down a few notches, though.

Gitte kept going at full speed after the divorce. In 1988, she and beefy New York Jets defensive end Mark Gastineau had a red hot transcontinental affair with trademark Gitte glitz. Flamboyantly partying and then posing for the press on both coasts, they became daring lovers. Announcing their engagement at an Italian restaurant in New York City in the spring, they sealed it by having each other's names permanently tattooed on their own rear ends. Don't believe it? Ask the patrons at Don and Charlie's Restaurant in Phoenix who Gitte and Mark mooned to show off their artwork.

The only one not laughing was Gastineau's wife, Lisa, who had filed for divorce a few months before. Seems Mark was still a married man, but Lisa told reporters that Gitte was welcome to him and she hoped they'd just go out and breed themselves their own football team.

Soon, it was revealed that Gitte was pregnant, but her publicist announced in June that she'd suddenly suffered a miscarriage while filming a movie in Italy. Gastineau rushed to her side. By July, their relationship had cooled. But, in the fall, Gastineau suddenly quit the Jets when he learned Gitte had been stricken with a form of cancer.

Gitte, by now an authority on getting her man, was asked by US magazine what man in the whole world she'd like to meet next. Her answer: the Pope. Runner up: Sting. Let's all follow that.

Jackie Stallone has kept busy, too. She was a judge at the 1988 Mr. and Miss Nude California Pageant and always has a few thoughts to share with the press. Displeased with her choices for President in 1988, Jackie said Sly should run. "If he ran tomorrow, he'd get it" she told Star interviewers. Better than that, she figured because he always ran his movie productions efficiently and on budget, there wouldn't be any national debt with him in the White House.

Since his split from Gitte, Sly hasn't exactly been locked in his room pining, either. First, he filmed his most grueling motion picture yet--Rambo III--where, on camelback in the Afghan desert, he fights Russian troops and tanks to rescue his pal, Col. Sam Trautman. Then, he turned his attention to his own social life and proved the Italian Stallion was back in action. In rapid fire order he wooed model Kathy Lynn Davis, Entertainment Tonight's Leeza Gibbons, George Hamilton's ex, Alana Stewart, blue-blood debutante of the decade Cornelia Guest, actress Helena Michaelson, Devin DeVasquez, Dena Goodmanson, Suzanne La Cock and Tess.

And, he's been dating Wheel of Fortune's Vanna White and even escorted her to the prestigious 1988 White House Correspondents' Dinner in Washington, D.C.

Sly's love life will always make headlines but there's so much more to him than his romantic escapades. Through hard work and true genius, he's moved millions of people with his films. He has given everyone so much in his life, it just doesn't seem fair that marital peace and contentment have eluded him and that his marriages have failed.

US magazine asked him how he figured it and how he wanted people to remember him. He replied that he had done "it the hard way and never let failure take him down. Failure only inspired me to work harder. So I'd like to think of myself as an underdog who made good."

Johnny Carson at the Beverly Hilton Hotel where the
California Friars Club honored Ed McMahon at their annual
stag roast. (Scott Downie, Celebrity Photo)

Chapter 20

Johnny Carson

He is Aunt Blabby, Art Fern, Floyd R. Turbo and Carnac The Magnificent. The undisputed King of late-night television, he's a friendly face in millions of bedrooms and living rooms across the country. While actor Robert Blake describes him as "the ace comedian top dog talk artist of the universe," most of the rest of us remember the night Joan Embry's marmoset monkey crawled to the top of his head, nervously perched there for a moment quivering at the camera and then relieved himself all over the famous star. He's been a million laughs. Everybody likes him . . . except his three ex-wives . . . and even they really should because Johnny Carson is also the famous signature line on their millions of dollars of alimony checks.

His marriages have marked passages in his show business career and suffered because of his work in television. His divorces have become a part of our culture.

The first one was friendly and quiet. Johnny and college sweetheart Jody Wolcott were married in Nebraska in 1949. He landed a job at an Omaha broadcast station, was a big hit and soon moved to Hollywood to try his hand in the big leagues of network television. Jody raised their three young sons out of the limelight in the couple's suburban ranch home while Johnny wrote comedy for Red Skelton. His first major starring role came in 1957 when ABC tapped him to host its new daytime *Who Do You Trust* program and moved him to New York to broadcast it. But the marriage of the shy Nebraska farm girl and the ambitious network TV star didn't survive--they separated in 1959 and later obtained a quicky Mexican divorce.

Johnny's rendezvous with destiny struck in 1962, when NBC selected him to replace Jack Parr as host of its popular *Tonight Show*. His next rendezvous was in 1963--with shapely airline stewardess Joanne Copeland; he married her in August of that year in New York City. During their marriage, Johnny was a *Tonight Show* workaholic who devoted every ounce of his energy to the show. It was hard work--writing fresh monologues, putting guests at ease with interesting questions and performing zany Mighty Carson Art Players' skits. But it paid off and Johnny became one of the most popular stars on television. The only ratings war he lost was at home--Joanne left after seven years.

While Johnny publicly accepted the blame for not spending as much time on their relationship as he did on his new show, his sentiments weren't sweet enough for Joanne. After a protracted divorce, she took him for nearly half a million dollars in cash and art and $100,000 a year in alimony for life. Interestingly, after the divorce, she went back to college and earned a Ph.D. in nutrition. Then, she hosted cable TV's *Alive and Well Show*. Sitting on that kind of alimony, why not CNN's *Money Line*?

At Johnny's request, NBC moved the *Tonight Show* to Hollywood in 1972. The change of scenery worked wonders and, in the sun and fun of California, he was rejuvenated and his enjoyment of life restored.

On September 30, 1972 the network hosted a lavish Los Angeles party for Johnny, Ed, Doc and all the *Tonight Show's* staff and crew to celebrate the 10th anniversary of the program since Johnny was named host. When his time came to make a few remarks, Johnny shocked everyone there by reporting that he'd already had a busy day ... he and former model Joanna Holland had been secretly married at 1:30 p.m. that afternoon.

Carson was 46, Joanna was 33 and during the next ten years of their lives they would enjoy the fruits of his labor as Johnny's career hurtled into hyperspace. Under his skillful nurturing, the *Tonight Show* attracted more than 15 million viewers each night and earned NBC more advertising revenues than any other single program. The network returned the favor by rewarding their most precious star with millions upon millions of dollars. From his beginning annual salary of $100,000, Johnny was given so many raises that by 1983 he was earning 1 1/2 million dollars a month. He now holds the record as the highest paid performer in the entire history of television.

The Carsons moved into a magnificent $5 million Bel Air mansion and Joanna's influence slowly began to show in her man. First, she convinced him to stop tinting his hair and let the natural gray be seen on the air. Then she tried to temper his workaholism and total devotion to his television show by getting him away from Hollywood. Introducing him for the first time in his life to European travel, he loved it so much he started looking for ways to get more time to enjoy it.

He went straight to the NBC brass and told them he deserved more time for himself. With the phenomenal popularity of his show, Carson was powerful enough to force NBC to shorten the program from 90 minutes to an hour in length and to reduce his workweek to four and, in some weeks, three nights a week. He demanded and received 15 weeks of vacation each year, too.

The years were platinum-lined and Johnny and Joanna literally lived better than the monarchs of some countries. They owned eight elegant homes across the country, including three different sumptuous apartments in New York City and vacation palaces in Palm Springs and Las Vegas. A Rolls Royce convertible, a Mercedes Benz 450 SLC and other luxury automobiles stocked their several garages. They traveled the globe, enjoyed every luxury and spent millions on themselves.

He called her "Babes," she called him "Sweetums," and life was grand.

But by 1980, the marriage was showing some wear. Joanna believed he was putting more energy into the *Tonight Show* than their marriage, and she hauled him to a marriage counselor. Over the next two years, it was reported she lost respect for him to the point that she finally kicked him out of the house. He unpacked his suitcases at their Malibu beach vacation home and waited for her to drop the divorce bomb. She did on March 8, 1983 in the Clerk of Court's office on the first floor of the Los Angeles County Courthouse.

The divorce battle that raged over the next two years would set many ignominious records, but what it boiled down to was one of the biggest money grabs ever made by a wife for her husband's income and assets. Joanna didn't just want to take Johnny to the cleaners, she wanted to leave him hanging on the clothesline out back.

> "My producer, Freddy de Cordova, really gave me something I needed for Christmas. He gave me a gift certificate to the legal office of Jacoby & Myers."

On September 13, 1983 Joanna filed an application in which she asked the Judge to order Johnny to pay her $220,000 per month in temporary alimony ($2.6 million a year) "in order that I can maintain my standard of living which I have enjoyed during the past several years." In addition, she demanded he pay $500,000 to her attorneys for their initial fees and send over $176,000 to her accountants and appraisers so they could begin the work of stripsearching Johnny's books.

She swore out a financial statement in which she said it cost her $107,000 a month just to pay her bills at home. Those monthly expenses included $4,945 in salaries for her servants, $1,400 for the month's groceries for herself, $690 for household supplies, an $800 telephone bill each month, $220 to gas up her cars, $2,695 each month for travel and vacations, $1,085 in limo tabs, $12,365 to buy gifts each month for friends, $3,955 to spend on clothing monthly at local department stores and $37,065 every month to buy jewelry and furs. Apparently quite the letter writer, she listed expenses of $120 a month for stationery. And, she included $5,915 for security. All totaled, she calculated her basic needs and expenses at $107,665 a month; rounded it off to $220,000 to take care of any taxes and carrying charges and insisted Johnny pay every penny of it.

In an affidavit accompanying her demands, she testified that Johnny was earning tremendous income from the Tonight Show--from $8.5 million in 1980, to $12 million in 1981 and now to $15 million in 1982. She wanted a clean 50% of it and her $220,000 a month, too. She argued the private security was necessary because Johnny kept cracking jokes on the show about her commandeering the home.

"Passed by my house yesterday--in a tour bus."

As a result, she explained, Johnny's fans were writing her nasty crank letters and some were even trying to scale the fence and invade the grounds. So, she needed a private security force.

She claimed that there were other mouths to feed and payroll checks to write, too, for her gardener, maid, cook, her personal secretary and an assistant who did her laundry. Now there's a staff. (At his home in Malibu, Johnny answered the door himself and didn't have a covey of servants waiting on him. He had only one houseman to help keep up the place.)

Another line item on Joanna's wish list was $2,500 per month in child support from Johnny for Tim Holland, her grown son by a previous marriage.

Joanna's accountants, the firm of Touche Ross, also filed an affidavit supporting her request for temporary litigation fees. They noted that Johnny had a financial interest in 29 different companies, including Johnny Carson Apparel, DeLorean Motor Co., and Carson Productions, and that it would take them over a thousand hours to get to the bottom of what he was really worth.

The accountants pointed out that Joanna was also demanding 50% of all of Johnny's company perks, such as the cars, travel and profit sharing NBC provides him, which would also require much time on their part to uncover and evaluate.

> [An old lady stopped him on the street.]
> "She says, 'Johnny, I want a divorce from you.' And I say, 'But we're not even married.' She says, 'Yeah, but I want to skip right to the goodies.'"

The court records reveal that in real life Johnny wasn't laughing--he was infuriated. He accused her of being the imperial ex, surrounding herself with several full-time servants to dote over her like she was the Queen of England. Finding her claimed expenses exaggerated, he scoffed that there was no way she could eat $1,400 worth of groceries in a month. Her claims for limousine services particularly riled him because he'd left her a Rolls Royce and a Mercedes in the garage and didn't think he should have to pay for limo travel on top of it.

Johnny declared:

> "In relation to our standard of living, it should be noted that Mrs. Carson's totally exorbitant demands are several-fold my own personal monthly expenses of approximately $19,500 plus $11,500 which I regularly spend each month on the support of my mother for nurses, maintenance, etc."

Johnny's attorneys backed him up with a biting brief filed with the Judge in which they attacked Joanna for trying to squeeze $220,000 a month out of him for such "highly questionable monthly expenditures" as the $7,333 cash draw, $12,365 for gifts and $4,900 for charity. Those demands were just "staggering" and revealed nothing more than her own "wasteful, extravagant [and] over-indulgent" spending.

On top of that, Johnny's legal muscle explained to the Judge that Joanna's claims were "wildly exaggerated." They denied flat out that she ever had monthly living expenses approaching $220,000, and said a CPA's review of the couple's books during the marriage revealed she typically spent only $30,000 a month.

Johnny's lawyers said she lavishly overspent on creature comforts for herself, including keeping an empty third condominium in New York City and overstaffing her home. Furious that she was demanding Johnny continue to pay her $37,000 a month for furs and jewelry after she kicked him out, they bristled that he had already bought her five new furs recently, including a fur-lined raincoat, and that her closets were bulging with an elegant wardrobe large enough to clothe several people in style. And, she already had $2 million worth of jewelry. She didn't need anymore!

Johnny and his lawyers also argued that Joanna was sitting on a $350,000 CD which was belching out huge interest checks to her and that she had a job as a fashion design consultant in New York where she was earning a handsome monthly salary of her own. With her own sources of income, Johnny didn't think it was fair for him to be held responsible for 100% of her needs and living expenses.

Johnny didn't like the idea of paying $500,000 to Joanna's attorneys, either. He said she was gorging herself on lawyers just like she did with all her other wild spending--she'd hired two law firms, 14 attorneys, 5 paralegals and two accounting firms to go after his ass(ets). One of her attorneys, Arthur Crowley, was charging her $260 an hour and $520 an hour when he worked on Sundays.

The idea of paying that much to Joanna's attorneys became even more repulsive to Johnny when they started putting the screws to him. While Joanna's application for temporary alimony and attorney fees was pending trial, her lawyers got rough. To get a handle on how much Johnny was really worth, they used the power of the court to demand all of his cancelled checks from 1980 to date, all his bank statements and savings account passbooks going back to 1972, and the books and ledgers of all his businesses. They made him answer 170 questions in writing and under oath about his income, assets and tax returns. Going straight to his prized *Tonight Show*, Joanna's attorneys ordered Johnny to turn over all of the program's ledgers, books, accounts, ratings, office logs and papers-- even those kept by producer Freddy de Cordova.

As a final insult, attorney Crowley insisted on sending his own appraisers to perform a proctoscopy on the books of Johnny's 18 different companies, including the Carson Broadcasting Company, The Anniversary Show Company and Carson Productions, Inc. The latter produces the *Tonight Show* and *Late Night with David Letterman*, and it was Crowley's gripe that owners of TV production companies often are able to lowball their actual net worth because such companies have no fixed assets like studios or equipment--they only create programs for television networks.

As a case in point apparently inserted to needle Johnny by a reference to his best friend and closest personal advisor, Henry ["Bombastic"] Bushkin, Crowley advised the Judge that he had represented Bushkin's wife, Judy, when she divorced Bombastic the year before. Bushkin owned 10% of Carson Productions and an expert accountant from Price Waterhouse valued his interest at $7,000 because the company owned virtually no tangible assets. In reality, Crowley noted, the wife's own appraiser valued it at $1.9 million and that was right on the money because the 10% share had paid Henry $710,000 in income in 1983 alone.

So, Crowley was telling Johnny that he was on to him and the ways of Hollywood producers to cover their assets. He also was signaling Johnny that he got his buddy Bushkin and he was going to get him next.

It must have been particularly painful for Johnny that they were going after his TV show, but it got worse. On the morning of Tuesday, October 18, 1983 he was forced to submit to several hours of adverse questioning by Joanna's attorneys in what's known as a deposition, or a cross-examination before trial by the opposing attorney which is under oath and transcribed by a court reporter. The questions were so hostile and the tenor so ugly that Johnny felt like he'd been in combat.

Two weeks later, he complained to the Judge that it was pure harassment for Joanna's attorneys to insist on scheduling things for him on the days he was working rather than during his days off. He told the Judge he was so unnerved by the attacks during his deposition that "it had a very definite negative impact on the quality of my performance that afternoon during the taping of *The Tonight Show*."

The star emphasized:

> "I would like the Court to appreciate that whatever economic success I (and my wife through our community) have enjoyed in the past is the result of a great deal of hard work on my part and the consistent quality of that work in performance after performance for many years. Notwithstanding what occurs in my personal life (or in court) I am compelled to go forward and tape the show. My mistakes ... are observed by millions of people."

He concluded with the request to the Judge to call off the pit bulls and at least spare him the "great ... personal distress" which Joanna's lawyers were trying to inflict on him.

> "I resolve that if I ever again get hit in the face with rice, it will be because I insulted a Chinese person."

The Judges started seeing it Johnny's way and he won three major victories in a row at the courthouse over the next several months.

ROUND ONE: On February 17, 1984 Judge Frances Rothschild called the warring attorneys into her chambers to discuss Joanna's application for $220,000 a month in temporary alimony. It was the Judge's opinion that $35,000 a month was a much more reasonable alimony amount, that Johnny should not have to pay Joanna's massive attorney fees at that time and that the couple should divide some of their liquid assets 50-50 to pay for their respective expenses until the final trial. In the Judge's presence, then, the attorneys struck an agreement on temporary matters which obligated Johnny to pay $35,000 a month in alimony and which divided $4 million in stocks and municipal bonds equally between the two.

ROUND TWO: After a lengthy hearing on July 13, 14 and 16, 1984 Judge William P. Hogoboom agreed with Johnny that the parties had legally separated on November

7, 1982 rather than the March 4, 1983 date Joanna claimed. Under California law, this was one of the most significant battles in the whole divorce because Johnny earned nearly $6 million between those two dates, and if the Judge ruled the later date was the point of formal separation, Joanna would be entitled to a 50% community property share of Johnny's $6 mil. So, this whole three day trial was limited to that one issue and Johnny and Joanna fought hard over it.

The fact was undeniable that Johnny took his personal belongings and moved to Malibu on November 7, 1982, but Joanna insisted they didn't stay completely separated after that time. Her evidence was that Johnny returned to the Bel Air mansion weekly to sign household expense checks, they spoke on the telephone frequently and they spent holidays together. Specifically, it was revealed that she invited Johnny to Thanksgiving dinner, that they spent two nights together at the Camelback Inn in Scottsdale, Arizona, in December, and that they celebrated Christmas together.

But as the trial progressed and Johnny's evidence was introduced, a far different picture emerged. Sure, she'd invited him over for Thanksgiving but he attended only on the condition that no one else be present and according to Johnny, she used the occasion to tell him what she wanted for Christmas. (It was their custom for her to select her gift each year and for him to pay for it later.) And, it was true the two of them had visited Johnny's ailing parents in Arizona and stayed in the same hotel suite, but they absolutely did not have sexual relations. Johnny also didn't deny seeing his wife at Christmas; but did she want him there to prepare him for the bill for the gift she'd picked out for herself? It had a $100,000 price tag, and he eventually paid it.

Johnny stated that Joanna told him on November 6, 1982: "I want you to get the hell out of my life." He replied: "You got it."

Judge Hogoboom ruled there was "overwhelming evidence of [an] intent to separate in November 1982."

"I went to see my butcher the other day,
Murray Giblets. I said, 'how do you pick
a good turkey?' And he says, 'You
ought to know. You're a three time
loser.'"

ROUND THREE: In December, 1984 less than ten
months after she was awarded $35,000 a month in tempo-
rary alimony, Joanna demanded that the Judge make
Johnny pay her $6,000 more each month. She complained
that she just couldn't make ends meet because her actual
monthly living expenses were $54,000; and without an in-
crease in alimony she'd have to dip into some of the $2 mil-
lion in stocks and bonds she got the last time the Judge
carved up Johnny's wallet.

She made a big production of trying to prove to the
Judge that her monthly expenses exceeded her alimony income, including swearing to an itemization of her bills
which indeed totaled $54,000 a month. But she went too far
and Johnny caught her. He cried foul when he saw her
claim of $270.38 a month for "pet care" on the list she gave
the Judge. When his turn came, Johnny set the record
straight that Joanna simply did not own a pet prior to their
separation, and it was news to him if she bought one since.
And he was outraged at the idea that he was financially responsible for the cat's support. On top of that, how could
you ever spend $270 a month on a cat? Use a mink-lined
litter box?

"I heard from my cat's lawyer. My cat
wants $12,000 a month for Tender Vittles."

Johnny asked that the Judge make Joanna "keep her
part of that [temporary alimony] bargain" and not let her
welsh on it now. He reminded the court that she got a cool
$2 million from him already in the deal and insisted that if
she spent more on herself each month than the $35,000 he
was paying in alimony, she should pay for it herself.

Judge Rothschild agreed and, on February 8, 1985, issued a terse one sentence order: "Petitioner's OSC [Order
to Show Cause] for increase of spousal support is denied."

Not only did Johnny's three interim courthouse victories
provide him some much needed damage control as he
weathered the divorce, but they also set the stage for a final
out-of-court settlement of the whole case. The only question remaining was exactly how the assets would be divided; and the parties agreed to an informal procedure
where retired L.A. Superior Court Judge Lestor Olson
would preside over negotiations between Johnny's and
Joanna's attorneys to resolve that issue. For the next four
weeks, Judge Olson conducted numerous conferences
between the attorneys as they fought tenaciously to divide
Johnny's great wealth.

Of course, millions and millions of dollars were at stake.
Joanna figured that during their ten-year marriage Johnny
had amassed $13 million in stocks and bonds, $8 million in
such businesses as Carson Broadcasting and Carson Productions, $4.5 million in such speculative ventures as cattle,
mining and precious metals, eight homes across the country from New York to Malibu worth $10 million, and luxury
automobiles, pricey art and an airplane worth $9.5 million.
There was also $3 million in cash.

As Judge Olson and the attorneys argued over the details, Johnny braced himself. He knew full well that under
California's community property laws, Joanna was entitled
to 50% of all the assets accumulated during the marriage
even though he was the one who worked and earned virtually 100% of the couple's income during that time.

The Judge and the attorneys went after Johnny's assets
like a blind dog goes after hanging meat. What emerged on
August 30, 1985 was an 80-page divorce settlement to
which Johnny and Joanna agreed. The meticulous document, approved by Judge Olson as the full and complete
resolution of all issues arising from the divorce, was more
detailed and much longer than the World War I Armistice
with Germany, the World War II Japanese and German In-
struments of Surrender, the 1782 treaty between England

and the American colonies ending the Revolutionary War, the Louisiana Purchase, the treaty of Ghent ending the War of 1812 and the United Nations Charter. . .combined.

In fact, Joanna got more money and more land than several nations have received from their vanquished after winning wars. In the real estate column, she was awarded the couple's mansion at 400 St. Cloud Road in Bel Air, the Hotel Pierre condominium in New York City, and apartments at 201 East 62nd Street and 910 5th Avenue in New York. To travel in style, she got the 1976 Rolls Royce, the 1976 Mercedes Benz and all the jewelry, clothing and furs purchased during the marriage.

Financially, she walked away with a lion's share of Johnny's fortune, including 310 shares in Carson Broadcasting Corporation stock, one-half of all the stock in the Albuquerque Broadcasting Corporation, $216,000 in cash from their tax refund and the couple's two Wells Fargo bank accounts. She got valuable RCA debentures, Signal Corporation stock, one-half of several of Johnny's companies, $388,000 in accounts receivable and 75 solid gold Krugerrands.

In addition, she was awarded $337,500 from the salary Johnny earned doing the annual *Tonight Show* Anniversary shows, a hefty chunk of Johnny's AFTRA and Screen Actor's Guild pensions and 50% of all the money NBC will pay Johnny in the future for airing re-runs of *Tonight Shows* which he starred in during the marriage.

Incredibly, Johnny was even ordered to pay Joanna $35,000 a month in alimony for five years--on the first of each month from September 1, 1985 to December 1, 1990. And in one final twist of the knife, it was ruled that if Johnny died anytime before December, 1990 he would still have to continue making those alimony payments even though he was dead . . . on time, each month, from his estate!

Johnny limped away with the crumbs that were left, but salvaged a few major assets as well. He got his 1984 and 1985 contracts with NBC, the legal right to use his name as a television personality and profit from it in the future without paying Joanna for it, and all the video equipment in his possession. He was allowed to keep his Malibu beach home, the Scottsdale, Arizona house, 36 acres of land in Dead Horse Canyon outside L.A., the Las Vegas property and the Trump Tower condo in New York.

He was given some of the money, too, including more than $1 million in CD's, 25 gold Krugerrands, all the stock in Johnny Carson Apparel and Carson Tonight, Inc., various other miscellaneous stocks and bonds, and his feed lot investment. He also got the 1973 Mercedes, 1979 Mercedes, 1985 Ford Bronco, 1939 Chrysler and all his television souvenirs and memorabilia.

But Johnny has learned how to cope with divorce-- rather than let it drag his life to a stop in a cesspool of self pity and remorse, let it mark a new beginning of better things to come. And that's exactly how it worked again for him after divorce number three.

His new life took several forms--in his contentment with the peacefulness of beach life as the Pacific lapped against his $9 million contemporary-style Malibu villa, renewed joy from his hobbies of astronomy, magic and practicing on his drum set at home, and his construction of a multi-million dollar Wimbledon-style tennis court in his yard so he could play his favorite sport more often.

One other new form completed the picture of Johnny enthusiastically embracing the future: a stunning young bikini-clad blonde named Alexandra Maas.

Some say the attractive stock brokerage secretary was actually stalking the newly single star as she walked back and forth along the beach in front of his home until he noticed her. But there she was anyway . . . strolling along the beach with an empty wine glass in her hand. When Johnny's hormones carried him outside to meet this luscious creature, she asked if she could borrow a cup of wine and he was hooked.

Fueled by his own zest for living, his eternal optimism, his belief in the institution of marriage and their love for each other, Johnny married Alex on June 20, 1987 at his Malibu home. Retired L.A. Circuit Court Judge William Hogoboom, who had presided over parts of Johnny's third divorce, performed the ceremony at Johnny's personal request. Only the Judge's wife, Betty, and Johnny's brother Dick were in attendance, as Johnny was absolutely determined to keep the wedding secret. He remembered only too well the disgusting media circus that had been Sean Penn and Madonna's wedding just the year before right next door to Johnny's home, with helicopter news crews dive bombing the service to take photographs.

He might be one of the country's most public figures and best known celebrities, but Johnny Carson is a very private person. He's even been described by friends as a loner. He simply took matters into his own hands and made sure no one knew.

> "You may think that my giving advice on
> marriage is like the captain of the Titanic
> giving lessons on navigation."

The simple ceremony was held under a sprawling tree in his lush yard as the Pacific provided the background music. Johnny had speakerphones installed in the yard and in the living room of Alex's parents back in Pittsburgh. Alex's Dad gave her away by phone and Johnny told them quietly, "I'll take good care of your daughter."

Johnny was 61 years old, Alex was 35, and a fresh, new start was underway in his life. They boarded Johnny's own private jet and flew to London where they honeymooned in an $800-a-night hotel suite. By day, the vivacious duo enjoyed the Wimbledon tournament from a VIP box and by night they dined and danced at the city's most fashionable clubs.

Johnny was so successful in keeping the wedding secret that nobody back in Hollywood knew about it until nine days later, while the couple was already on their honeymoon. The thrice-burned comedian also reportedly took another precaution for this fourth marriage--he asked Alex to sign a prenuptial agreement limiting her take at less than 50% of his net worth in the event they ever divorced. But nobody wants to think about that grim possibility now, especially seeing how radiant Johnny is with young Alex and how happy he is to be starting a new life at his age.

Johnny Carson has had three marriages end in failure, has been hatefully dragged through some very ugly divorce mud and has been stripped of his life's savings and possessions. But each time an ex and her lawyers knocked him down, he refused to stay down. And all the while, he kept the rest of us laughing.

Question: What would you like on your epitaph?

Answer: "I'll be right back."